Volume 17, Number 2

D0286687

2002

Contents

Subscriber Information

Journal of Mass Media Ethics (ISSN 0890–0523) is published quarterly by Lawrence Erlbaum Associates, Inc., 10 Industrial Avenue, Mahwah, NJ 07430–2262. Subscriptions for the 2002 volume are available only on a calendar-year basis.

Printed journal subscription rates are $35.00 for individuals and $320.00 for institutions within the United States and Canada; $65.00 for individuals and $350.00 for institutions outside the United States and Canada. Order printed subscriptions through the Journal Subscription Department, Lawrence Erlbaum Associates, Inc., 10 Industrial Avenue, Mahwah, NJ 07430–2262.

Electronic: Full price print subscribers to Volume 17, 2002 are entitled to receive the electronic version free of charge. Electronic-only subscriptions are also available at a reduced price of $288.00 for institutions and $31.50 for individuals.

Change of Address: Send change-of-address notice to Journal Subscription Department, Lawrence Erlbaum Associates, Inc., 10 Industrial Avenue, Mahwah, NJ 07430–2262.

Claims for missing issues cannot be honored beyond 4 months after mailing date. Duplicate copies cannot be sent to replace issues not delivered due to failure to notify publisher of change of address.

Journal of Mass Media Ethics is abstracted or indexed in *Communication Abstracts; Communication Institute for Online Scholarships; Columbia Journalism Review; ComIndex; Media and Values; Nordicom Finland; Public Affairs Information Service; Com Abstracts; Humanities Index; Humanities Abstracts;* EBSCO*host* Products.

Microform copies of this journal are available through ProQuest Information and Learning, P.O. Box 1346, Ann Arbor, MI 48106–1346. For more information, call 1–800–521–0600, ext. 2888.

Requests for permission should be sent to the Permissions Department, Lawrence Erlbaum Associates, Inc., 10 Industrial Avenue, Mahwah, NJ 07430–2262.

Journal of Mass Media Ethics, 17(2), 87–88
Copyright © 2002, Lawrence Erlbaum Associates, Inc.

Foreword

In this issue of the *Journal of Mass Media Ethics* we revisit the topic of ethics codes in the media. We explored codes thoroughly in 1985–1986, when the journal first appeared. In the intervening years we have published occasional research articles on the subject. Now, given myriad code revisions and debates over enforcement throughout media associations and individual media institutions, this is an optimum time to return to the subject. Four articles and a Cases and Commentaries section inform the debate.

Kathy Fitzpatrick of DePaul University has been a thoughtful student of public relations ethics. From her recent experience in helping the Public Relations Society of America (PRSA) revise its code she brings an insider's view into an organization struggling with its credibility and standards. She offers us two articles. The first traces the first 50 years of PRSA's code writing and code enforcement experiences. Most of the versions of the PRSA code between 1950 and 2000 made pleas for professionalism and offered largely ineffective enforcement provisions. Fitzpatrick's second article shows how the 2000 Member Code of Ethics assumes professional standing for PRSA members, emphasizes public relations' advocacy role, and stresses education rather than enforcement as the key to improving industry standards. The multiphase process PRSA has undertaken is instructive, as is the inclusion of that code and all previous PRSA codes in Fitzpatrick's articles.

Our third article, by Yehiel Limor of Tel-Aviv University and Inés Gabel of Israel's Open University, traces the evolution of the Israel Broadcasting Authority's (IBA) code of ethics through five permutations between 1972 and 1998. The authors question whether the code is the outcome of a search for ethical and professional guidelines or a means of protecting the IBA from external pressures. Since 1972 the code has become more detailed, reflecting ethical, organizational, and political sensitivities. The authors conclude that the result of these changes has been the crystallization and implementation of normative ethical guidelines for Israeli public broadcasting.

Taegyu Son of the University of North Carolina at Chapel Hill then analyzes how journalistic codes of ethics in the United States wrestle with the matter of leaks. After assessing how leaks—particularly from government sources—can compromise journalistic independence, the article discusses strengths and weakness of ethics codes. Four research questions are explored via a systematic analysis of 47 codes. Although leaks are never explicitly addressed in these codes, the treatment of confidential sources and the need to maintain journalistic independence are addressed.

The Cases and Commentaries section explores the ethical ramifications of a public relations practitioner's decision about presenting a false front group or grassroots image as a part of a public relations campaign. Four commentators wrestle with how the PRSA code and fundamental ethical principles can be brought to bear when Machiavellian supervisors ask the public relations person to help sway public and political opinion.

Finally, two book reviews stimulate further thought about entertainment media ethics and ethics in cyberspace. Lawrence Wenner of Loyola Marymount University pens a lengthy review of F. Miguel Valenti's *More Than a Movie: Ethical Decision Making in the Entertainment Industry*. He finds the book to be a somewhat shallow text for film school students, but a rather interesting exploration of an important media function that scholars only rarely consider. And John Ferré reviews Cees Hamelink's *The Ethics of Cyberspace*, a call for universal access to cyberspace, respect for human rights, and participatory democracy, which Ferré finds to be "high ideals certainly, and high priced ones, too." *JMME* readers may be intrigued with Hamelink's dismissal of deontological and teleological theories.

The Editors

Journal of Mass Media Ethics, 17(2), 89–110

Evolving Standards in Public Relations: A Historical Examination of PRSA's Codes of Ethics

Kathy R. Fitzpatrick
DePaul University

❏ *The Public Relations Society of America (PRSA) adopted its first code of ethics in 1950, 2 years after PRSA was formed. During the next 50 years, the code was revised and updated several times to keep pace with industry practices and increased expectations for ethical performance. In 2000 a new code was adopted to heighten awareness of ethical issues and address concerns regarding code enforcement. In this article I trace the 50-year evolution of PRSA's codes of ethics and related code-enforcement activities.*

Front groups, conflicts of interest, nondisclosure, unfair competition, representation of dubious clients, deceptive practices, gifts to the media, failure to safeguard confidential information: These are some of the ethical issues for which public relations professionals often are criticized. The list has not changed much in the 75 or so years during which public relations has grown into a thriving profession, and neither has the field's efforts to curb such practices.

A self-regulated industry, public relations must rely on its practitioners to determine appropriate standards of conduct. And it must rely on the same practitioners to police their peers in the shared effort to uphold ethical standards. In this regard, the Public Relations Society of America (PRSA or the Society), frequently acknowledged as the industry's leading association, historically has taken the lead.

Two years after the Society was formed in 1950, PRSA wrote its first code of professional standards to address the shared "responsibility for the good character and reputation of the public relations profession" (PRSA, 1950b, p. 8). During succeeding years, the code was revised several times and a somewhat elaborate enforcement process added. In 2000 a new code was adopted to heighten awareness of ethical issues and address concerns regarding code enforcement.

In this article I trace the 50-year evolution of PRSA's codes of ethics and related code enforcement activities. The article is based on reviews of academic and professional literature pertaining to public relations ethics generally and PRSA codes of ethics specifically; archival documents and reports related to PRSA's codes of ethics and provided by PRSA; and personal communication with select current and former PRSA leaders, members of PRSA's Board of Ethics and Professional Standards (BEPS or Ethics Board) and BEPS' legal counsel.

Evolving Codes of Ethics

More than half a century ago, PRSA adopted its first code of ethics on December 4, 1950, at its third annual meeting. Although general in content and vague in practical guidance, the brief document laid the groundwork for future codes and established the direction of its successors. It emphasized serving the public interest; avoiding conflicts of interest; communicating honestly; avoiding misrepresentations to clients, employers, and others; and the continuing professional development of public relations practitioners (PRSA, 1950a).

According to Homer N. Calver (1951), then chairman of the PRSA Committee on Standards of Professional Practice, the code was part of PRSA's effort to enhance the professional standing of public relations, "a major objective in the formulation of the Society" (p. 3). Apparently a compromise among PRSA members, some of whom wanted no code at all, the new code also was a reaction to perceptions of misbehavior on the part of public relations practitioners. Calver noted, "Some glaring examples of questionable ethical practice have been already commented on by members. Everyone hopes, of course, now that we have a code, similar practices will entirely disappear" (p. 3).

PROFESSIONAL STANDARDS
for the
PRACTICE OF PUBLIC RELATIONS

As members of the Public Relations Society of America, we subscribe to the belief that inherent in the practice of public relations is the obligation of a public trust which requires fulfillment of these principles:

1. Objectives which are in full accord with the public welfare as well as the interests of our clients or employers;
2. Accuracy, truthfulness and good taste in material prepared for public dissemination and in all other activities sponsored, partici-

---

pated in or promoted, whether as independent public relations counsel or as officer or employee of a trade association, company or other
organization or group;

3. Standards of practice which preclude the serving of competitors concurrently except with the full knowledge and consent of all
concerned; which safeguard the confidential affairs of client or employer even after termination of professional association with him
and so long as his interests demand; and which, with full regard for
our right to profit and to advance our personal interests, nevertheless
preserve professional integrity as the primary concern in our work;

4. Cooperation with fellow practitioners in curbing malpractice
such as the circulation of slanderous statements or rumors, the concealment from clients or employers of discounts or commissions, or
any other information to which they are entitled; and deliberative
distortion or misrepresentation for professional gain or competitive
advantage;

5. Support of efforts designed to further the ethics and technical
proficiency of the profession and encourage the establishment of adequate training and education for the practice of public relations.

We realize full well that interpretation of a Code of Ethics becomes
a matter of personal judgment in many instances, but we hold that a
sincere effort to implement the spirit of the above principles will as-
sure professional conduct of credit to the profession and honest service to clients and employers.

PUBLIC RELATIONS SOCIETY OF AMERICA

Adopted by the membership December 4, 1950
Reprinted with permission of the Public Relations Society of America.

A strong proponent of code enforcement mechanisms as additional
"influence to discourage malpractice," Calver (1951, p. 3) encouraged
PRSA to develop enforcement provisions that would strengthen the code
and improve industry practices. In 1954 PRSA took his advice, revising
the original code and amending its bylaws to include provisions for enforcing PRSA's new standards of performance. The revised code—often
cited as PRSA's first code—included fewer words, added one principle,
and read more like a pledge than its predecessor. As described at the
time, "strong emphasis is placed on public relations being *a profession
with standards of practice*" (PRSA, 1955, p. 8). PRSA's membership then
numbered 1,139.

PROFESSIONAL STANDARDS
for the
PRACTICE OF PUBLIC RELATIONS

As members of the *Public Relations Society of America*, we share a responsibility for the good character and reputation of the public relations profession. Therefore we pledge ourselves to make a sincere effort to adhere to the following principles and standards of practice:

1. We will keep our objectives in full accord with the public welfare
   as well as the interests of our clients or employers.
2. We will be guided in all our activities by the standards of accuracy, truth, and good taste.
3. We will safeguard the confidence of both present and former clients or employers.
4. We will not engage in any activity in which we are directly or indirectly in competition with a present client or employer without
   the full knowledge and consent of all concerned.
5. We will cooperate with fellow practitioners in curbing malpractice.
6. We will support efforts designed to further the technical proficiency of the profession and encourage the establishment of adequate training and education for the practice of public relations.

   To the extent that we live up to these principles and standards of
practice, we will be meeting our responsibilities for making the
profession in which we are engaged worthy of continued public
confidence.
   (The Professional Standards for The Practice of Public Relations
were revised by the Board of Directors of the Public Relations Society
of America, at the St. Louis Board Meeting, October 15–16, 1954.)

Reprinted with permission of the Public Relations Society of America.

1959 Code Stressed Enforcement

Almost 10 years after PRSA's first code of ethics was written, the Society
adopted a much broader code that amplified concepts in the earlier models
and included two paragraphs directly related to enforcement. The new
provisions required members to serve if called as a witness in an enforcement proceeding and to "co-operate with fellow members in upholding
and enforcing this Code" (PRSA, 1959). Perhaps because ethical accountability had become increasingly important to Society leaders, the drafters

of the 1959 code placed more weight on "improper" (Watson, 1960, p. 23) activities than on ethical best practices, relying heavily on the phrase "shall not."

The new standards introduced a "duty of fair dealing" with clients, employers, and others; added prohibitions against the corruption of communication channels, third-party organizations, contingency fees, encroachment on other members' employment, and derogatory actions toward other members' clients, employers, or their products, business, or services; and required members to terminate relationships that required actions that would violate the code (PRSA, 1959). The 1959 code established a model that would remain in place for more than 40 years.

PROFESSIONAL STANDARDS
for the
PRACTICE OF PUBLIC RELATIONS

Public Relations Society of America

This Code was adopted in November 1959 by the 1960 PRSA Board of Directors and ratified by the 1960 PRSA Assembly. It replaces and strengthens a similar Code of Professional Standards for the Practice of Public Relations previously in force since 1954.

Declaration of Principles

Members of the Public Relations Society of America acknowledge and publicly declare that the public relations profession in serving the legitimate interests of clients or employers is dedicated fundamentally to the goals of better mutual understanding and cooperation among the diverse individuals, groups, institutions and elements of our modern society.

In the performance of this mission, we pledge ourselves:

1. To conduct ourselves both privately and professionally in accord with the public welfare.
2. To be guided in all our activities by the generally accepted standards of truth, accuracy, fair dealing and good taste.
3. To support efforts designed to increase the proficiency of the professional by encouraging the continuous development of sound training and resourceful education in the practice of public relations.
4. To adhere faithfully to the provisions of the duly adopted Code of Professional Standards for the Practice of Public Relations, a copy of which is in the possession of every member.

Code of Professional Standards
for the
Practice of Public Relations

This Code of Professional Standards for the Practice of Public Relations is adopted by the Public Relations Society of America to promote and maintain high standards of public service and conduct among its members in order that membership in the Society may be deemed a badge of ethical conduct; that Public Relations justly may be regarded as a profession; that the public may have increasing confidence in its integrity; and that the practice of Public Relations may best serve the public interest.

1. A member has a general duty of fair dealing towards his clients or employers, past and present, his fellow members and the general public.

2. A member shall conduct his professional life in accord with the public welfare.

3. A member has the affirmative duty of adhering to generally accepted standards of accuracy, truth, and good taste.

4. A member shall not represent conflicting or competing interests without the express consent of those concerned, given after a full disclosure of the facts.

5. A member shall safeguard the confidences of both present and former clients or employers and shall not accept retainers or employment which may involve the disclosure or use of these confidences to the disadvantage or prejudice of such clients or employers.

6. A member shall not engage in any practice which tends to corrupt the integrity of channels of public communication.

7. A member shall not intentionally disseminate false or misleading information and is obligated to use ordinary care to avoid dissemination of false or misleading information.

8. A member shall not make use of any organization purporting to serve some announced cause but actually serving an undisclosed special or private interest of a member or his client or his employer.

9. A member shall not intentionally injure the professional reputation or practice of another member. However, if a member has evidence that another member has been guilty of unethical, illegal, or unfair practices, including practices in violation of this Code, he should present the information to the proper authorities of the Society for action in accordance with the procedure set forth in Article XIII of the Bylaws.

10. A member shall not employ methods tending to be derogatory of another member's client or employer or of the products, business or services of such client or employer.

11. In performing services for a client or employer a member shall not accept fees, commissions, or any other valuable consideration in connection with those services from anyone other than his client or employer without the express consent of his client or employer, given after a full disclosure of the facts.

12. A member shall not propose to a prospective client or employer that his fee or other compensation be contingent on the achievement of certain results, nor shall he enter into any fee agreement to the same effect.

13. A member shall not encroach upon the professional employment of another member unless both are assured that there is no conflict between the two engagements and are kept advised of the negotiations.

14. A member shall, as soon as possible, sever his relations with any organization when he believes his continued employment would require him to conduct himself contrary to the principles of this Code.

15. A member called as a witness in a proceeding for the enforcement of this Code shall be bound to appear unless, for sufficient reasons, he shall be excused by the panel hearing the same.

16. A member shall co-operate with fellow members in upholding and enforcing this Code.

Reprinted with permission of the Public Relations Society of America.

PRSA's bylaws were amended in concert with the development of the 1959 code in an effort to enhance code enforcement. The new bylaws provided for a system of due process that involved a national judicial council consisting of judicial panels of six judges each, with one panel serving each of PRSA's districts. The panels heard complaints of code violations, held hearings on alleged violations, and made recommendations to censure, suspend, expel, or exonerate an accused party. PRSA's Board of Directors had ultimate authority in deciding cases.

The judicial panels relied on PRSA members to bring potential code violations to the attention of panels in their respective districts, in effect, charging members with the policing of their peers. PRSA leaders urged members to take seriously their "moral responsibility" (Decker, 1963, p. 10) to participate in code enforcement proceedings and to enhance professional practices. "Members of the Society can take pride in the first firm steps taken in the direction of ethical practices and they should take patient hope that they are on the sure path of progress toward an ethical profession" (Decker, 1963, p. 10).

Grievance Board Established in 1962

The work of the judicial panels was supplemented in 1962 with the establishment of a 9-member Grievance Board (renamed the PRSA Board of Ethics and Professional Standards in 1983), which served as a "watchdog" for the Society to investigate complaints by nonmembers or situations in which violations may have occurred but complaints were not filed by members (McKee, 1971). The Grievance Board's charge was to bring appropriate cases before the judicial panels and to prosecute the same (McKee, 1971). In other words, the Grievance Board served as the "prosecutor," which decided whether to file a charge—regardless of how a violation was brought to its attention—and the judicial panels served as the "juries" once a case was filed (Smith, 1973). According to early PRSA leaders, this approach was based in part on the Society's review of similar processes used by legal, or bar, associations. (For a more detailed explanation of the grievance process, see Decker, 1963.)

The PRSA bylaws provided that no publicity be given to the actions of the Grievance Board.

Because all proceedings of both the Grievance Board and judicial panels were confidential and conducted in closed sessions, PRSA members learned of alleged violations only if the PRSA Board of Directors adopted a resolution of censure, suspension, or expulsion, all of which required notice to members. In cases involving a decision by a court of law, the Society would take no action until a court decision was rendered. The PRSA bylaws provided that no publicity be given to the actions of the Grievance Board (McKee, 1971).

1963 Code Revision

PRSA continued to refine its code, and in 1963 notable changes were made in Paragraphs 4 and 8. Paragraph 4 was expanded to strengthen the prohibition on conflicts of interest: " ... nor shall he place himself in a position where his interest is or may by in conflict with his duty to his client, employer, another member or the public without a full disclosure of such interests to all concerned" (PRSA, 1963b). More significant was the effort to address growing concerns about the use of front groups (i.e., third-party organizations formed to advance the undisclosed special interests of clients or employers). Paragraph 8 was split into new paragraphs 8 and 9, reading as follows:

8. A member shall be prepared to identify to the public the source of any communication for which he is responsible, including the name of the client or employer on whose behalf the communication is made.

9. A member shall not make use of any individual or organization purporting to serve or represent some announced cause, or purporting to be independent or unbiased, but actually serving an undisclosed special or private interest of a member or his client or employer. (PRSA, 1963b)

Code Interpretations Added

In the same year, PRSA's Financial Relations Committee, working with PRSA's legal counsel and the Securities and Exchange Commission (SEC), prepared "An Official Interpretation of the Code as It Applies to Financial Public Relations." In brief, the 1963 interpretations provided that financial relations counselors were ethically bound to know, and act within, SEC and other rules and regulations and laws related to financial communications; to follow generally a "full disclosure" policy of corporate information; to maintain "confidential" information; to exercise "reasonable care" to ascertain and disseminate "accurate" information; "to act promptly to correct false or misleading information or rumors"; to clearly identify "sources" of communication, including the name of the client or employer represented; to avoid conflicts of interest; and "to maintain the integrity of channels of public communication" and "standards of good taste" (PRSA, 1963a).

In 1966 official interpretations of the code were developed to clarify selected paragraphs and provide examples of prohibited behaviors (see PRSA, 1966). The interpretations were intended to serve as advisory opinions regarding proper professional conduct in public relations (Decker, 1963). Again, this procedure was "adapted from the practice of bar associations which have found it desirable to authorize one of its committees to issue advisory opinions on professional ethics" (Decker, 1963, p. 3).

An "Official Interpretation" for political public relations was later added, requiring members "to be conversant with" and to adhere strictly to the laws and regulations governing political activities (PRSA, 1973). The provisions noted that although "partisan advocacy on behalf of a candidate or public issue may be expected," members should not "issue descriptive material or any advertising or publicity information or participate in the preparation or use thereof that is not signed by responsible persons or is false, misleading, or unlabeled as to its source"; and members should not "through the use of information known to be false or misleading, conveyed directly or through a third party, intentionally injure the public reputation of an opposing interest" (PRSA, 1973).

"Misdemeanor" Violations

In 1970, the PRSA Board of Directors expanded the authority of the Grievance Board to take action in troublesome, but minor, cases that did not warrant full investigations. In such instances, the board could warn members who had allegedly violated the code that "continuance of the performance in question could result in serious consequences" (PRSA, n.d.). Three years later, the PRSA board further expanded the policy to include other cases in which "the importance of the matter was not proportionate to the time, money and effort required for a judicial hearing" (PRSA, n.d.).

In such misdemeanor cases, the Grievance Board could authorize legal counsel to write the accused member, identify the alleged infraction, and request an explanation. On receipt of the explanation, the Grievance Board could drop the matter if the explanation warranted and notify the member that "although the case is not of sufficient importance to prosecute, that notice of the misdemeanor is being recorded in his confidential file at PRSA headquarters and that any further infractions of the Code could result in a full scale case" (PRSA, n.d.).

Code Revision Spurred
by the Federal Trade Commission

In 1977 PRSA's code came under scrutiny by the Federal Trade Commission (FTC) as part of an FTC investigation of voluntary codes of trade and professional associations. The FTC advised PRSA that it considered Paragraph 14, which banned the "encroachment" of one member on the employment of another, to be a restraint of competition, and Paragraph 13, which banned contingency fees, to be a form of price fixing. Facing the possibility of a formal complaint by the FTC, PRSA deleted the provisions (Schorr, 1977). A new provision was added to replace the ban on contingency fees, reading as follows: "A member shall not guarantee the achievement of specified results beyond the member's direct control" (PRSA, 1977a). The changes primarily affected independent public relations counselors who at that time comprised about 20% of PRSA's 8,337 members (PRSA, 1977b).

The deletions were made in conjunction with other adjustments to the code that year. The Declaration of Principles included new references to the importance of constitutional and human rights. A more significant change was the deletion of the requirement that members "not employ methods tending to be derogatory of another member's client or employer or of the products, business or services of such client or employer" (PRSA, 1977a). Other deletions included the provision requiring that members "cooperate with fellow members in upholding and enforcing the Code," as well as the code's sexist language (PRSA, 1977a).

1988 Code Revision

The 1977 code remained in effect until the 1983, when relatively minor revisions in language and format were made to clarify various concepts. In 1988 the code was expanded to 17 paragraphs, or articles, which included several noteworthy amendments (PRSA, 1988).

> *The 1988 code was the first to acknowledge specifically a member's "dual obligations to client or employer and the democratic process."*

The 1988 code was the first to acknowledge specifically a member's "dual obligations to client or employer and the democratic process" (PRSA, 1988). The provision regarding service to the "public interest" became the first article (suggesting higher value; PRSA, 1988). Concepts related to truthful communication received greater attention, with three separate articles stressing, respectively, the importance of "honesty and integrity," the importance of "accuracy and truth," and the avoidance of disseminating "false or misleading information" (PRSA, 1988). The prohibition on engaging in practices intended to corrupt channels of communication was expanded to include " … or processes of government" (PRSA, 1988). The code placed new emphasis on the responsibility to avoid personal conflicts of interest. And the provision regarding a duty to safeguard confidences was expanded to include "privacy rights" of present, future, and prospective clients or employers (PRSA, 1988).

PROFESSIONAL STANDARDS
for the
PRACTICE OF PUBLIC RELATIONS

This Code was adopted by the PRSA Assembly in 1988. It replaces a Code of Ethics in force since 1950 and revised in 1954, 1959, 1963, 1977, 1983.

Declaration of Principles

Members of the Public Relations Society of America base their professional principles on the fundamental value and dignity of the individual, holding that the free exercise of human rights, especially freedom of speech, freedom of assembly, and freedom of the press, is essential to the practice of public relations.

In serving the interests of clients and employers, we dedicate ourselves to the goals of better communication, understanding, and cooperation among the diverse individuals, groups, and institutions of society, and of equal opportunity of employment to the public relations profession.

We Pledge:

To conduct ourselves professionally, with truth, accuracy, fairness and responsibility to the public;

To improve our individual competence and advance the knowledge and proficiency of the profession through continuing research and education;

And to adhere to the articles of the Code of Professional Standards for the Practice of Public Relations as adopted by the governing Assembly of the Society.

Code of Professional Standards
for the
Practice of Public Relations

These articles have been adopted by the Public Relations Society of America to promote and maintain high standards of public service and ethical conduct among its members.

1. A member shall conduct his or her professional life in accord with the public interest.

2. A member shall exemplify high standards of honesty and integrity while carrying out dual obligations to a client or employer and to the democratic process.

3. A member shall deal fairly with the public, with past or present clients or employers, and with fellow practitioners.

4. A member shall adhere to the highest standards of accuracy and truth, avoiding extravagant claims or unfair comparisons and giving credit for ideas and words borrowed from others.

5. A member shall not knowingly disseminate false or misleading information and shall act promptly to correct erroneous communications for which he or she is responsible.

6. A member shall not engage in any practice which has the purpose of corrupting the integrity of channels of communications or the processes of government.

7. A member shall be prepared to identify publicly the name of the client or employer on whose behalf any public communication is made.

8. A member shall not use any individual or organization professing to serve or represent an announced cause, or professing to be independent or unbiased, but actually serving another or undisclosed interest.

9. A member shall not guarantee the achievement of specified results beyond the member's direct control.

10. A member shall not represent conflicting or competing interests without the express consent of those concerned, given after a full disclosure of the facts.

11. A member shall not place himself or herself in a position where the member's personal interest is or may be in conflict with an obligation to any employer or client, or others, without full disclosure of such interests to all involved.

12. A member shall not accept fees, commissions, gifts or any other consideration from anyone except clients or employers for whom services are performed without their express consent, given after full disclosure of the facts.

13. A member shall scrupulously safeguard the confidences and privacy rights of present, former, and prospective clients or employers.

14. A member shall not intentionally damage the professional reputation or practice of another practitioner.

15. If a member has evidence that another member has been guilty of unethical, illegal, or [engaged in] unfair practices, including those in violation of this Code, the member is obligated to present the information promptly to the proper authorities of the Society for action in accordance with the procedure set forth in Article XII of the Bylaws.

16. A member called as a witness in a proceeding for enforcement of this Code is obligated to appear, unless excused for sufficient reason by the judicial panel.

17. A member shall, as soon as possible, sever relations with any organization or individual if such relationship requires conduct contrary to the articles of this Code.

Reprinted with permission of the Public Relations Society of America.

In 1990 the PRSA Counselors Academy developed special interpretations of the code for members of public relations firms. The interpretations stressed "an overriding responsibility to carefully balance public interests with those of their clients, and to place both those interests above their own," and it required that members operate "in an open and truthful manner at all times" (PRSA, 1990). The interpretations emphasized the need for members to "protect the integrity" of their business relationships; to "exert best efforts" to satisfy the requirements of clients; to employ the "highest ethical business practices" in purchasing activities; to avoid using or sharing "inside information"; and to avoid gaining competitive advantage through the payment or receipt of "extraordinary gifts, gratuities, or other favors" (PRSA, 1990).

These interpretations, along with those for financial and political professionals, remained in effect until the 2000 code was adopted. In hindsight, one might conclude that instead of clarifying the ethical guidelines, PRSA's continuing efforts to improve the code through interpretations contributed to members' confusion regarding acceptable—and unacceptable—behavior. Judith Cohen (personal communication, July 3, 2001), legal counsel to the Ethics Board for almost 20 years, recalled the difficulty of construing and applying the code—even for BEPS members. "In some instances, there was no dispute about the facts [of a case]. Rather it was simply a decision of whether the facts fit the code" (J. R. Cohen, personal communication, July 3, 2001).

The Challenge of Code Enforcement

In the 50 years since PRSA adopted its first code of ethics, the issue that has sparked the most discussion and debate is enforcement. Although members historically expressed strong support for a "code with teeth," they also expressed little confidence that the PRSA code had any (Ramey, 1973). The fact that relatively few formal sanctions were handed out over the years most likely contributed to such attitudes.

> *Although members historically expressed strong support for a "code with teeth," they also expressed little confidence that the PRSA code had any.*

According to a PRSA (1989) research report on the history of code enforcement, 200 cases were presented to the Grievance Board or judicial panels between 1952 and 1989 (the last year in which a formal report was prepared). Reportedly, more than half of the cases were brought to the board as a result of newspaper articles, and the rest were presented by members and nonmembers. Only one case was filed directly with a judicial panel (PRSA, 1989). A sample of the complaints illustrates the nature and complexity of the issues addressed:

1952–1969

- Mail fraud
- Tax evasion
- Soliciting another member's client
- Conspiracy
- Suppression of information
- Failure to register as a foreign agent
- Misrepresentation to client
- Release of inaccurate information
- Guaranteeing results
- Use of "front" organization
- Plagiarism
- Misrepresentation of credentials
- Libel
- Contract dispute
- Improper "finder's fee"

1970–1979

- Misleading press release
- Soliciting the client of another member
- Bribery of government official
- Guaranteeing specific results
- Making derogatory remarks about a public relations professional
- Acceptance of improper fees
- Use of "front" organization
- Marketing a defective product
- Conflict of interest
- Misrepresentation to client
- Issuance of false statement regarding stock value
- Income tax evasion
- Overstated earnings
- Illegal campaign contributions
- Invasion of privacy
- False advertising
- Violations of a political campaign act
- Sexual discrimination

- Restraint of trade
- Contingency fee arrangement
- Embezzlement
- Receiving kickbacks

1980–1989

- Derogatory references about other public relations firms
- Involvement in a prostitution ring
- Guaranteeing media placements
- Malpractice
- Copyright infringement
- Unfair dealing with journalists
- Improper use of APR [accredited in public relations] mark
- Breach of contract
- Dissemination of misleading information
- Misrepresentation of facts
- Issuance of false news release
- Soliciting another member's client
- Embezzlement
- Plagiarism
- Breach of confidentiality
- Insider trading
- Failure to reveal source of funding for political campaign materials
- Representation of competing interests without consent
- Unfair treatment of employees
- Improper business solicitations

According to the report, approximately 65% of the cases were investigated (PRSA, 1989); 10% of the cases involved nonmembers, and 12% involved court or SEC decisions, which precluded the Grievance Board from taking immediate action. "The remaining cases were either informally investigated by the Grievance Board or were acted upon by a panel" (PRSA, 1985, p. 10). As of 1989, judicial panels had heard 34 cases (PRSA, 1989). In 6 cases, the accused members resigned while the case was in progress, thereby precluding further action by PRSA. The completed investigations reportedly resulted in two expulsions, two suspensions, three censures, three reprimands, and one admonishment. One should note that the report also states that "several cases were treated under the misdemeanor provisions, and in several other cases letters of admonition were sent to the accused" (PRSA, 1989, p. 8). Why only one "admonishment" was included in the formal tally of case resolutions is unclear, however. The rest of the cases were dismissed, withdrawn, or settled without a hearing.

Although a formal report on enforcement activities during 1990 to 2000 is not available, individual case reports and correspondence with BEPS's legal counsel indicate that 31 cases were considered during that period (J. R. Cohen, personal communication, May 15, 2001). All of the cases ultimately were closed without action. Four of the accused members resigned during investigations. In 9 cases, BEPS sent letters to the accused parties indicating some concern with their conduct but took no further action. In one case, which arose out of a court action, BEPS reportedly monitored the case and took no action after the lawsuit was settled.

Thus, according to available data, during the first 50 years in which the PRSA code was in effect, only 11 of 231 cases considered (with at least 65% investigated) resulted in formal sanctions against members for unethical behavior. If letters of admonishment or concern are included, the number of enforcement "actions" is at least double that figure, although PRSA records do not include the total number of such letters. Notably, 6 of the 11 sanctions occurred prior to 1973 and resulted from findings of a court of law rather than the findings of PRSA judicial panels (PRSA, 1989). This means that five formal sanctions were imposed against members as a result of PRSA investigations from 1954 to 2000. Unless one assumes that most of the allegations were groundless, the PRSA enforcement system was clearly ineffective in adjudicating ethical misconduct.

Unless one assumes that most of the allegations were groundless, the PRSA enforcement system was clearly ineffective in adjudicating ethical misconduct.

Some former PRSA leaders dispute such a conclusion. James A. Little, former chair and 10-year member of BEPS and 1981 PRSA president, said he finds such statistics "a little misleading" (J. A. Little, personal communication, July 2, 2001). Stressing that the enforcement "process *did* work," Little observed that the biggest problem associated with code enforcement was confidentiality. Even members of PRSA's Board of Directors did not fully understand the work of BEPS, according to Little. "When I was chair of BEPS, we did an awful lot of work which nobody knew about and nobody should have known about," he said. There was "never a word said to membership, never a word said to the press" (J. A. Little, personal communication, July 2, 2001).

PRSA leaders' confidence in the enforcement system was buttressed by pride in PRSA's position as the only public relations association to have an enforceable code. According to 1973 PRSA President Betsy Ann Plank (personal communication, June 18, 2001), "The enforcement aspect of the code was a distinctive pride-and-joy of PRSA leaders—certainly this one. We often declared that PRSA is the only public relations professional organization which has established means for enforcement of a code of ethics."

Despite such championing, many PRSA members—most of whom favored ethical accountability—remained skeptical about code enforcement efforts (McKee, 1971). A 1973 research study documented their lack of confidence in PRSA's judicial process. Almost half of the respondents to a survey of PRSA leaders, including chapter presidents and chairs of the judicial panels and the Grievance Board, reported that they

> did not believe the present PRSA ethical machinery—both codes and enforcement—was sufficiently effective. The main reasons for this attitude were: the weak enforcement of code violations; the code's inability to relate to non–PRSA members; and that many Society members are not willing to "blow the whistle" on other members. (Ramey, 1973, p. 16)

In response, PRSA leaders reminded members that because participants in the judicial process could not speak about enforcement activities, members may have falsely perceived that PRSA was not actively pursuing code investigations (Smith, 1973). They shared members' frustration about the lack of authority over nonmembers. And they chastised members for their unwillingness to participate in the enforcement process.

Dean G. Grogan, who spoke on behalf of PRSA to the Georgia Chapter in 1972, preempted the release of the survey's findings in a presentation tellingly titled, "Let's Clear the Cloud of Doubt of the Clout of the Code." Stressing both the importance of member involvement in the process and the confidential nature of grievance procedures, Grogan said, "Because Grievance Board members do not discuss their work, there seems to be a tendency to think the Board is doing nothing" (Grogan, 1972, p. 2). Additionally, he said, the majority of complaints brought to the attention of the Grievance Board involved nonmembers over which PRSA had no jurisdiction. And, he said, members who faced accusations of unethical behavior could simply resign from PRSA and avoid further involvement. Finally, Grogan explained, the code's enforcement provisions were designed to punish those who "intentionally" engaged in unethical behavior, not those who simply expressed bad judgment (p. 2).

Rea W. Smith (1973), who helped draft the 1959 code and who for many years handled the PRSA staff work associated with ethics cases, also expressed strong support for the Code's enforcement provisions. At PRSA's

1973 Spring Assembly meeting, Smith emphasized that any concerns regarding lack of code enforcement could be attributed directly to members' lack of involvement in the enforcement process. "The membership cannot have it both ways—they cannot be critical of code enforcement if they, as individuals, don't want to 'get involved.' ... So don't blame the police or the courts if the victims refuse to file complaints" (Smith, 1973, p. 3).

Franco Case Illustrates Enforcement Challenge

One widely publicized case in 1986 provides an example of the challenges related to code enforcement. The incident involved PRSA's then-president Anthony M. Franco, the owner of a public relations firm. The SEC accused Franco of violating the SEC's insider trading regulations in a stock transaction involving one of his clients. After settling the case through a consent decree, by which he neither admitted nor denied wrongdoing, Franco resigned his position as PRSA president—but not his membership in PRSA—and voluntarily appeared before the PRSA Ethics Board (PRSA, 1986).

According to John W. Felton (personal communication, June 22, 2000), then president-elect and in line to succeed Franco when the BEPS proceedings began, PRSA was "muzzled" from addressing the matter publicly by the confidentiality provisions of PRSA's bylaws. As a result, PRSA was sharply criticized in the news media for its handling of the case (Bernstein, 1986). To make matters worse, PRSA members were outraged that PRSA officials appeared to be doing nothing to address the situation. Again, because of the confidentiality requirements of the code enforcement system, PRSA officials could make no public statement about their actions. Before the issue was resolved, several chapters "threatened to leave PRSA" (J. W. Felton, personal communication, June 22, 2001).

According to Felton,

> the other element which made this a nightmare for us was that a consent decree ... is not an admission or denial of guilt or innocence ... [so] the burden of proof was ours. To prove guilt we as a Society would have to start from scratch to collect and introduce evidence that the accused actually committed the charges—a long and costly process. (personal communication, June 22, 2001)

In the end Franco resigned from PRSA in the midst of the BEPS investigation, effectively closing the case (PRSA, 1986). Again, PRSA made no public comment. In addressing PRSA's Assembly the following month, Felton said that although

> many believed that the [PRSA] Board failed to take strong enough action ... if we broke the rule of confidentiality for a member who resigned under inves-

tigation or pending charges, that member could bring legal action for anything defamatory contained in a statement made by the Society. (J. W. Felton,
personal communication, June 22, 2001)

Felton ultimately succeeded in soothing PRSA members' concerns and
later called for a change in the bylaws to avoid similar incidents in the future. As a result, the PRSA Board of Directors adopted new guidelines requiring disclosure by PRSA board nominees, candidates, elected officials,
and staff of matters that might reflect adversely on the PRSA (J. W. Felton,
personal communication, June 22, 2001). At the same time, no changes
were made in the code enforcement process.

A New Code in 2000

Perhaps as a result of an increasingly negative ethics climate in U.S. institutions (Seib & Fitzpatrick, 1995) in the late 1980s and early 1990s, PRSA
created several task forces to address issues of ethics (see e.g., PRSA, 1992).
In 1993 PRSA introduced a new strategic plan, which called for PRSA to become by the year 2000 "the standard bearer for ethical business practice"
(Warner, 1973, pp. 2–3). Although no immediate code-related actions were
taken, these initiatives suggest that ethics had become a priority for PRSA.

Concurrently, in an increasingly litigious environment, the code enforcement situation had worsened. PRSA members accused of code violations often refused to provide evidence related to their conduct, relying on
legal counsel to handle their communication with the Ethics Board (R. D.
Frause, personal communication, June 11, 2001). According to Cohen (personal communication, July 3, 2001), when members refused to turn over
information needed to prove a code violation, BEPS could do little. Unlike
in a court of law, no sanctions were available for noncompliance. Additionally, the potential for defamation lawsuits related to BEPS proceedings
was always a concern. "One massive lawsuit would be the end of PRSA,"
Cohen said.

After repeated requests from BEPS for PRSA to consider changes in the
existing standards (Fitzpatrick, 2002; R. D. Frause, personal communication, June 11, 2001; J. A. Little, personal communication, July 2, 2001), the
PRSA Board of Directors held an Ethics Summit with members of the Ethics Board to discuss the code and the enforcement process. Following this
meeting in early 1999, the PRSA board gave BEPS the go-ahead to develop
a new code.

The next year, BEPS presented a new code of ethics to PRSA Assembly
delegates (representing PRSA chapters) at the 2000 national conference.
With their approval, the code became effective on that day, October 21, 2000.

(For a detailed report on the development of the PRSA 2000 Member Code of Ethics, see the second article in this issue of *JMME*, Fitzpatrick, 2002.)

> *... The 2000 code reflects the drafters' belief that the 50-year journey toward professional standing for PRSA members has been achieved.*

Unlike its predecessors, the new code included essentially no enforcement provisions (PRSA, 2000). Rather, it was designed to be aspirational and educational, such that prohibitions were replaced with positive, affirmative obligations (Fitzpatrick, 2002). The 2000 code emphasized the need for "responsible advocacy," stressing loyalty to clients and employers (PRSA, 2000). It also accentuated the importance of professional competence. Perhaps most significantly, the 2000 code reflected the drafters' belief that the 50-year journey toward professional standing for PRSA members had been achieved (Fitzpatrick, 2002).

Acknowledgment

I thank the University of Florida College of Journalism and Communications for its support of this work.

References

Bernstein, J. (1986, October 27). The Franco fiasco—the wages of sin. *Advertising Age*, p. 8.

Calver, H. N. (1951, February). Now that we have a code. *Public Relations Journal*, pp. 3–4, 17.

Decker, F. K. (1963, April). The path towards professionalism: PRSA's code and how it operates. *Public Relations Journal*, pp. 7–10.

Fitzpatrick, K. R. (2002). From enforcement to education: The development of PRSA's 2000 Member Code of Ethics. *Journal of Mass Media Ethics, 17,* 111–135.

Grogan, D. G. (1972, July 6). *Let's clear the cloud of doubt of the clout of the code.* Paper presented at a meeting of the PRSA Georgia Chapter, Atlanta, GA.

McKee, J. E., Jr. (1971, June). The PRSA Grievance Board. *Public Relations Journal*, pp. 18–21.

Public Relations Society of America. (n.d.). *Functions and responsibilities of PRSA's Grievance Board.* New York: Author.

Public Relations Society of America. (1950a). *Professional standards for the practice of public relations.* New York: Author.

Public Relations Society of America. (1950b). *Public Relations Society of America register.* New York: Author.

Public Relations Society of America. (1955). *Public Relations Society of America register.* New York: Author.

Public Relations Society of America. (1959). *Professional standards for the practice of public relations.* New York: Author.

Public Relations Society of America (1963a). *An official interpretation of the PRSA Code of Professional Standards for the Practice of Public Relations as it applies to financial public relations.* New York: Author.

Public Relations Society of America. (1963b). *Professional standards for the practice of public relations.* New York: Author.

Public Relations Society of America. (1966). *Official interpretations of the code.* New York: Author.

Public Relations Society of America. (1973). *An official interpretation of the code as it applies to political public relations.* New York: Author.

Public Relations Society of America. (1977a). *Professional standards for the practice of public relations.* New York: Author.

Public Relations Society of America. (1977b, August 18). *News release.* New York: Author.

Public Relations Society of America. (1985). *History of enforcement 1952–1985.* New York: Author.

Public Relations Society of America. (1986, October 6). *News release.* Retrieved June 16, 2001, from PR Newswire on the LEXIS–NEXIS Academic Universe database.

Public Relations Society of America. (1988.) *Code of professional standards for the practice of public relations.* New York: Author.

Public Relations Society of America. (1989). *Grievance Board research report.* New York: Author.

Public Relations Society of America. (1990). *Counselors Academy's Interpretations to the PRSA code of professional standards.* New York: Author.

Public Relations Society of America. (1992, October 9). *Report of the PRSA task force on ethics board confidentiality.* New York: Author.

Public Relations Society of America. (2000). *Public Relations Society of America member code of ethics 2000.* New York: Author.

Ramey, E. (1973, Spring). Ethics—a bite or a blessing? *Forum,* p. 16.

Schorr, B. (1977, March 4). Public Relations Society draws fire of FTC over code. *Wall Street Journal,* p. 1.

Seib, P., & Fitzpatrick, K. R. (1995). *Public relations ethics.* Fort Worth, TX: Harcourt Brace.

Smith, R. W. (1973, May 4). *PRSA code enforcement.* Paper presented at the meeting of the PRSA Assembly, Des Moines, IA.

Warner, H. W. (1973, January). Blueprint 2000 aims to establish public relations as a strategic management tool. *Public Relations Journal,* pp. 15–16.

Watson, B. (1960, October). Whither the Society's code? Urgently needed—understanding of the new code and its enforcement. *Public Relations Journal,* pp. 23–26.

Journal of Mass Media Ethics, 17(2), 111–135

From Enforcement to Education: The Development of PRSA's Member Code of Ethics 2000

Kathy R. Fitzpatrick
DePaul University

❏ *The Public Relations Society of America's (PRSA) Member Code of Ethics 2000 assumes professional standing for PRSA members, emphasizes public relations' advocacy role, and stresses education rather than enforcement as key to improving industry standards. Code development involved more than 2 years of research and writing and the counsel of outside ethics experts. In this article I review the code development process, providing an insider's perspective on the ethics initiative.*

Public Relations Society of America (PRSA or the Society) members marked the new millennium by adopting a new code of ethics approved by PRSA's Assembly in October 2000 (see Appendix). The code, which replaced standards of practice established half a century ago and revised several times since, reflects the Society's desire to position PRSA as the ethics brand leader in the industry and to raise the ethical performance of public relations professionals (S. L. Waltz, Jr., personal communication, June 12, 2001).

PRSA's newest code differs from its predecessors in three significant ways. The 2000 code assumes professional standing for PRSA members; it emphasizes public relations' advocacy role; and it contains no enforcement provisions. In the words of code drafters, the code is aspirational and educational, designed to motivate ethical behavior rather than punish ethical misbehavior (R. D. Frause, personal communication, June 11, 2000). The code also is a reflection of changing times and the increased expectations for professional responsibility in public relations.

This article traces the development of PRSA's Member Code of Ethics 2000. It is based on research PRSA's Board of Ethics and Professional Standards (BEPS or Ethics Board) and the Ethics Resource Center (ERC) conducted; archival reports and correspondence related to PRSA's codes of ethics; personal communication with BEPS members and BEPS legal counsel; and personal communication with selected current and former PRSA leaders. The work also records the observations of the author, who has been a member of PRSA's Ethics Board for almost 6 years and participated in writing the 2000 code of ethics.

A New Code

Two primary factors influenced PRSA's decision to write a new code of ethics: recognition that the existing standards were no longer sufficient for addressing contemporary issues and practices and the need to address growing concerns related to code enforcement (PRSA, 2000c; R. D. Frause, personal communication, June 11, 2001; S. D. Pisinski, personal communication, July 2, 2001; and S. L. Waltz, Jr., personal communication, June 12, 2001). According to Robert Frause, BEPS chairman for 10 years and the leader of the code development process, the punitive nature of the existing code was a significant factor. "The existing code was no longer acceptable or appropriate because the focus was not on ethical public relations practices. The focus was on whether someone committed a violation and whether he or she should be sanctioned" (R. D. Frause, personal communication, June 11, 2001).

Of some additional significance was the perceived need to enhance the credibility of the public relations field. PRSA leaders were concerned about a 1998 study that found Americans ranked the public relations field last in credibility among 42 job categories or functions (ERC, 1999b). Although a new code of ethics alone could not change such perceptions, it could help raise the standard for ethical performance, according to PRSA leaders (S. L. Waltz, Jr., personal communication, June 12, 2001).

Serious discussions about code revision began in 1998, when the PRSA Ethics Board requested a formal meeting with the PRSA Board of Directors to address problems related to the PRSA Code of Professional Standards and Practices (last revised in 1988). As the group responsible for investigating potential violations of the PRSA code, BEPS members were particularly concerned with enforcement matters. (For a detailed discussion on the problems related to PRSA code enforcement, see the preceding article in this issue of *JMME*, Fitzpatrick, 2002). Frause (personal communication, March 17, 1999) outlined their views in a memorandum to the PRSA Board:

> Over the past three to six years the Board of Ethics and Professional Standards has confronted what we believe is a serious change in attitudes of PR practitioners in general as well as PRSA members specifically, regarding ethical practices and standards. What we have experienced is an eroding regard for PRSA's Code of Ethics and Professional Standards. What used to be clear violations of the code now go unresolved due to numerous loopholes in the way the code is written, administered and supported by the organization's

leadership and members as well. We believe the once dominant belief that PRSA's ethics code had meaning and was strictly enforced is now defunct.

Our experience now reveals that members who are accused of ethical misconduct employ attorneys and legal counsel who make mincemeat of violation accusations as they relate to our current code. BEPS' limited powers to gather information make it even more difficult to discover the truth and take action. Pure and simple, our entire committee is frustrated, powerless and unable to do justice to the spirit of the PRSA Code of Ethics and Professional Standards. We believe it is time for all of us to roll up our sleeves and pursue a meaningful code of ethics and professional standards that will work for the Society now and in the years to come.

Convinced by BEPS that some action was needed, PRSA officials scheduled a "Summit on Ethics" and contracted with the nonprofit ERC to undertake a preliminary study of the PRSA code and recommend improvements (R. D. Frause, personal communication, June 11, 2001). As part of its assessments, the ERC (1999b) interviewed leading public relations professionals, held a focus group with 8 to 12 public relations professionals, and surveyed 300 public relations practitioners.

> *The [existing] code was outdated, incomplete, too detailed, not clearly or cleanly written, operational rather than aspirational, too limited in terms of explanations, and provided no positive incentives for compliance.*

The ERC presented its report at the summit held in early 1999 during a regularly scheduled meeting of the PRSA Board of Directors. The research (ERC, 1999b) supported BEPS's proposal for a new code. Most compelling was the preliminary finding that PRSA members believed that PRSA's code was largely ineffective. At the same time, members were concerned that eliminating the enforcement provisions entirely would be a mistake. Several reasons—some contradictory—were cited for why the code was considered inadequate. According to the research participants, the code was outdated, incomplete, too detailed, not clearly or cleanly written, operational rather than aspirational, too limited in terms of explanations, and provided no positive incentives for compliance.

Concerns related to "spin," business practices, and professionalism also were raised through the research (ERC, 1999b). One interviewee suggested that "in some ways, lying permeates everything we do" (p. 5). Participants also cited billing, human resources, conflicts of interest, and marketing issues as problematic.

The ERC (1999b) recommended that the PRSA code "be rewritten and its enforcement provisions revised as part of a larger campaign to position PRSA as the integrity leader in the public relations field" (p. 1). As part of the process, the ERC suggested a comprehensive assessment of issues that should be addressed in the new code and the development or enhancement of ethics expertise on the part of code drafters and PRSA staff who would support the new code.

The summit proved to be the turning point in PRSA's decision to proceed with a new code of ethics. Although PRSA leaders were hesitant to concede that code enforcement was not working, they recognized the need to update the existing code, and they agreed that ethics should be the hallmark of PRSA membership (R. D. Frause, personal communication, June 11, 2001). BEPS and PRSA officials subsequently agreed that a new code of ethics—rather than simply a revision of the existing model—was needed to reflect the professional status and obligations of contemporary practitioners and to address the enforcement challenge.

Researching the Code

The code development process began with more research. Although members who had served on the Ethics Board for many years had some strong opinions regarding the type of code needed (i.e., one with less emphasis on code enforcement and sanctions and more emphasis on inspiration and encouragement), they felt involving PRSA members in the process was important. According to Frause (personal communication, June 11, 2001),

> Research confirmed what was intuitively known by BEPS' members but not really known by the rest of PRSA leadership, staff and members. Research also helped legitimize the findings and build consensus for approval by the Assembly. It showed that BEPS had done its homework and that the recommendations were based on relevant information.

Early in the research process, Frause sent a memo to PRSA board members, chapter presidents, Assembly delegates, and section/district chairs requesting their participation in a national discussion about the PRSA code (ERC, 2000b). The correspondence posed questions directly related to the development of a new code, including code structure and format, as well as substantive issues the Ethics Board had encountered during years of code-related investigations.

The ERC (2000b) received 20 responses from PRSA leaders. Participants said that having a code was important for the profession and for the future of PRSA. They also supported a revised code, with most supporting enforcement and suggesting that various degrees of punishment be used. Respondents also supported ethics education as an important reinforcement, noting that it was PRSA's responsibility to educate, guide, and lead its members and nonmembers regarding ethical practices. Respondents said that PRSA members should be held responsible for the actions of non–PRSA members they supervise and should identify employers, clients, and front groups.

Focus Group Findings

ERC representatives and PRSA Assembly delegates conducted focus groups at the October 1999 PRSA national conference. Approximately 240 PRSA members participated in 18 focus groups.

Focus group participants expressed strong support for revising the existing code and for professional ethical practices, with many supporting the use of PRSA resources to review the code and increase the focus on ethics (ERC, 1999a). Education on ethics also was supported, but views differed on the extent to which PRSA should commit resources for such efforts. Participants said that enforcement was desirable although it may not be practical. They also expressed some concern regarding the PRSA board's authenticity in support of ethical issues.

> *… the most critical or central ethics-related issues in the public relations industry involve truthfulness, the corruption of communication channels, and competitive practices.*

According to focus group participants, the most critical or central ethics-related issues in the public relations industry involve truthfulness, the corruption of communication channels, and competitive practices (ERC, 1999a). In addressing the ways in which dishonest business activities manifest themselves in public relations, participants cited the following concerns:

Truthfulness in Business Activities

- "Spinning" a message in a manner that may distort the truth about an issue or product.

- Clients who knowingly mischaracterize an issue or product to their public relations firms.
- Misrepresentation of a client.
- Front groups that advocate the position of a particular organization or issue without disclosing that they are doing so.
- Billing a client as if work had been done by a senior staff person when it was actually done by a junior staff person; padding of bills.
- Conflicts of interest created by firms' lack of disclosure regarding relationships with client competitors or other conflicts.

Corruption of Communication Channels

- Paying for editorial coverage.
- Sharing insider information.
- Sharing confidential/proprietary information.
- Advocating for a particular issue or product rather than dispensing information.
- Gift-giving or receiving in a way that creates undue influence.
- Media practices that distort channels of communication.

Competitive Practices

- Competitive intelligence practices that border on espionage.
- Intentionally damaging the reputation of a competitor or opposing side.
- Pressure from clients to bend rules, be unethical, or guarantee results.
- Pressure from leadership to bend rules, be unethical, or guarantee results.
- Pressure from marketing to bend the truth, be unethical, or guarantee the results.

In addressing the structure of a new code, focus group participants cited four features they found lacking in the existing code: clarity, simplicity, specificity, and teeth (ERC, 1999a). With regard to content, participants said the code should be "relevant" (p. 8). Commonly cited issues that should be addressed included the economics of ethics (i.e., the fact that taking an ethical stand might mean losing a job); licensing or certifying public relations professionals; effective enforcement mechanisms; "globalism" (p. 8); Internet activities; disclosure and confidentiality; front groups; and dealings with the media.

Focus group participants indicated a range of ideas on how the Ethics Board should draft a new code. Some suggested that PRSA members should participate in the process; others cautioned against "writing by committee" (ERC, 1999a, p. 8). With regard to code philosophy, most of the participants favored a positive approach focused on best practices rather than punishment. Commonly cited issues that should be addressed included whether members should sign a commitment on admission to PRSA, renewal of membership, or both; the role of judicial panels (PRSA bodies that decide cases involving alleged code violations); how to incorporate ethics into the member accreditation process; and ways for PRSA to "brand" (p. 9) the code and make members, clients, and the public aware of its existence.

In its preliminary research, the ERC had found that although many PRSA members believed code enforcement would remain largely ineffective without state licensing of practitioners, the enforcement "provisions were worth retaining, since eliminating them entirely would be a step in the wrong direction and would send the wrong signal to all public relations practitioners and others" (ERC, 1999b, p. 3). The focus groups seemed to support this finding, although participants were split in their views on whether enforcement was desirable, possible, or both (ERC, 1999a). Some thought a code "with teeth" (ERC, 1999a, p. 9) was the key to increased professional standing; others believed that even if enforcement were desirable it probably was not possible.

The ERC (1999a) found "no consensus and some disagreement" (p. 10) regarding the resources that PRSA should devote to ethics education and training. But "the simplicity of some [participants'] suggestions—mentioning ethics in standard communications—is a real indication that PRSA is in the beginning stages of integrating ethics into its organizational fabric" (p. 10). Participants' recommendations included ethics seminars and classes, affiliations with other organizations, the development of ethics resources (e.g., speaker's bureau and case studies, code compliance mechanisms, external promotion of PRSA values, integration of ethics into PRSA materials, and encouragement for members to include the code in routine practices, such as including it as part of proposals and contracts).

Survey Results

Using data gathered from the focus groups and preliminary research, the ERC developed and administered a survey of PRSA members in January 2000. The objectives were to gain additional insight into members' views on PRSA's mission, the organization's leadership, the current code, and the ethical climate in their workplace (ERC, 2000a). Initial and follow-up mailings of a 79-item questionnaire were sent to PRSA's 20,266 members. A total of 2,099 responses were received, for a response rate of 10.4%.

Key findings related to code development include the following (ERC, 2000a):

PRSA and Ethical Standards

- A sizable majority (92%) strongly agreed that ethics is a key part of PRSA's mission.
- Most (86%) agreed that PRSA's commitment to the highest ethical standards adds value to PRSA membership.
- Most agreed that PRSA' has a responsibility to set (87%), develop (92%), and uphold (92%) professional standards.
- Ninety-one percent believe that members' commitment to a code of ethics can help brand PRSA as a leader in ethical conduct.
- Only half (50%) believe that the professional and ethical standards of PRSA are higher than the standards of the industry as a whole.
- Fewer than half (46%) said they would turn to PRSA for guidance if faced with unethical or disturbing situations in the workplace.

Enforcement and Education

- Ninety percent agreed that PRSA should deny or revoke membership for failure to meet code standards.
- Ninety-two percent believe that a formal mechanism should be in place to resolve allegations of ethical misconduct.
- Eighty-five percent believe that PRSA should offer some form of education, counseling, or mediation to help members meet code standards, although only 57% said they would participate in PRSA ethics and professional standards training.
- Seventy-one percent believe that PRSA should invest financial resources in establishing a code of ethics, and 66% said PRSA should spend money to apply a code.

PRSA Code of Professional Standards for the Practice
of Public Relations

- Seventy-two percent said they had read the existing code within the past 2 years; academics and accreditation candidates were most likely to have read it.
- Most members strongly agreed (91% or higher) with most of the statements in the current code, although some ambivalence, uncertainty, or both were noted with respect to provisions related to appearing as a witness in a code-related hearing; identifying publicly the name of a client or employer; not accepting fees, commissions, and gifts from

nonclients for client-related work; severing relations with organizations or individuals requiring conduct contrary to the code; reporting unethical, illegal, or unfair practices; and conducting life in accord with the public interest.

When asked to share perceptions about the ethical climates in which they work, half of the members surveyed said they "feel an extraordinary amount of pressure to compromise their [ethical] standards" (ERC, 2000a, p. 23). Fifty percent said that they felt pressure from within their own organizations, and 40% reported feeling pressure from clients. About one third (34%) reported observing misconduct, and more than half (53%) of those respondents said they reported observed misconduct.

> *... half of the members surveyed said they "feel an extraordinary amount of pressure to compromise their [ethical] standards."*

Of considerable importance to BEPS throughout the research process were findings related to PRSA leaders' and members' attitudes regarding code enforcement and ethics education. Thus, in addition to the preliminary and formal research, the ERC posed three questions to PRSA Assembly delegates (who represent and vote in Assembly proceedings on behalf of PRSA chapter members). The survey questions and responses, as reported by the ERC (2000a, p. 27), follow:

1. "Should PRSA's Code of Professional Standards be coupled with a provision for strong enforcement or voluntary compliance?" Responses: evenly divided.
2. "Do you believe [PRSA] should invest in an ethics education program for our members and our external audiences, our clients and our employers? For example, do you believe [PRSA] should invest in an ethics education program for members and external audiences?" Responses: yes.
3. "Ethical practice is our most powerful brand difference as a society. Do you see ethics as a brand differentiator for PRSA?" Responses: evenly divided.

Writing the Code

Unless otherwise noted, this section reports the observations of Kathy R. Fitzpatrick, who participated in the development of the new code. Other members of the 2000 PRSA Board of Ethics and Professional Standards were David M. Bicofsky, Roger D. Buehrer, Linda Welter Cohen, James Frankowiak, Robert D. Frause (Chair), Jeffrey P. Julin, James E. Lukaszewski, and James W. Wyckoff.

When the research phase concluded, the ERC reiterated its earlier recommendation for PRSA to rewrite its code of ethics and develop the infrastructure and resources needed to support ongoing efforts related to ethics (ERC, 2000b). According to the ERC, a critical part of the package would be a communications and training strategy, as well as practical materials, to educate PRSA members and potential members about ethics matters. The ERC also stressed that PRSA leaders would have to support any new code both philosophically and financially.

The ERC's recommendations provided the basis for the code-drafting process to begin and proved valuable in developing the format of the new code:

> The revised code should have a strong aspirational framework that uses the PRSA mission as its foundation … [and] include a concise set of core professional principles that are aspirational in nature, references to detailed code provisions, and a clear statement on enforcement. The core principles in the revised code must clearly articulate those aspects of ethical conduct that are critical in public relations; and their relevance to members must be demonstrated. (ERC, 2000a, p. 29)

Body of Professionals

In anticipation of their first drafting session, BEPS members reviewed the research reports, as well as various codes of ethics and literature pertinent to the philosophical and practical aspects of code development. They joined ERC representatives in Washington, D.C., in April 1999 to begin a process that would take months to complete. The code drafters were guided by the same view of public relations that influenced the development of PRSA's early codes: "a profession with standards of practice" (see Fitzpatrick, 2002, p. 91).

At the same time, a significant difference can be noted in the historical and contemporary approaches to code development. Although they referred to public relations as a "profession," the drafters of PRSA's earlier standards viewed the code as a vehicle to help practitioners achieve professional standing (see Fitzpatrick, 2002). The 2000 drafters assumed that PRSA members had professional status.

This distinction became clear as the group addressed a critical first question posed by the ERC: Was PRSA a "professional body" or a "body of professionals?" ERC representatives had counseled earlier that although public relations practitioners are not "professionals" per se because of the lack of common learning and organizational structures, such deficiencies did not necessarily defeat the practice as a profession.

> From an ethical perspective, what defines a profession is not exclusively why people in the field act but also how they act. To be in a profession, or to be a professional, means both exercising technical skills (how one acts), which public relations practitioners certainly have, and serving society (why one acts). ... In a word, a professional must be pro-social. (ERC, 1999b, p. 6)

In fact, the question proved an easy one for BEPS members. Few debated that PRSA represented a "body of professionals" and that the new code should serve as a guide for the conduct of individual PRSA members. The group also agreed that the code should be based on ideals of professional ethics and responsibility. Thus, an important step was identifying the professional values that should guide contemporary public relations practice.

Articulating Values

A more challenging task was deciding what values should be included in the code. The drafters began by listing values important to all professionals and then adding those specific to public relations. As the list grew, so too did the difficulty in choosing among them.

Mindful that PRSA members wanted a clear and concise code and that fewer core values most likely would produce a more powerful document, the drafters narrowed the list. After much discussion and debate, they settled on six core values: advocacy, honesty, expertise, independence, loyalty, and fairness. As the code states, BEPS members believed that these values would set the industry standard for the professional practice of public relations. "These values are the fundamental beliefs that guide our behaviors and decision-making process" (PRSA, 2000a).

Honesty and *fairness* were viewed as ideals that reflect not only traditional public relations values but also the ethical counsel long provided by practitioners to clients and employers. Their inclusion in the code as core values reflects BEPS' belief in the ethical practitioner's respect for human rights and commitment to informed decision making in a democratic society.

The selection of *advocacy* and *loyalty* as core values both acknowledges and emphasizes the role of public relations professionals as representatives of special interests in the "marketplace of ideas." The balancing of private and public concerns—an issue that code drafters paid a great deal of attention to—was addressed semantically with the phrase "responsible advocacy" (PRSA, 2000a). The belief that public relations professionals best serve the public interest—as do other professionals—by responsibly serving their clients' and employers' interests is reflected in the statement, "We serve the public interest by acting as responsible advocates for those we represent" (PRSA, 2000a).

This provision also addresses the historical debate about how public relations practitioners should weigh the sometimes competing interests of clients and employers and those affected by public relations decisions. The new code's indication that loyalty to client or employer is paramount is a significant step in clarifying the professional role of public relations practitioners.

> *The new code's indication that loyalty to client or employer is paramount is a significant step in clarifying the professional role of public relations practitioners.*

The value of "independence" also reflects the professional stature of public relations by emphasizing the obligation of public relations professionals to provide sound, objective counsel unbiased by personal or other special interests. The term *objective* suggests that a public relations professional—similar to other professionals—should offer expert advice free of outside influences and in the best interest of the client or employer.

Finally, "expertise"—noted by at least one BEPS member as being more of a characteristic of a profession than a value per se—stresses the importance of professional competence. Certainly, special expertise is the hallmark of any profession, and it was deemed of such significance in this field to warrant special "core value" status.

Code Provisions

BEPS members believed that the professional values should be supported by principles designed "to affirmatively illustrate to practitioners what is expected of them as they practice the profession" (PRSA, 2000c, p. 26.) In this regard, the Ethics Board attempted to go beyond the behavioral guidelines common to many codes and address "why" one should act in specific ways. Such an approach, BEPS hoped, would provide greater direction for members in their daily decision-making processes. As a result, the new code's provisions address six important practice concepts:

- Free flow of information.
- Competition.

- Disclosure of information.
- Safeguarding confidences.
- Conflicts of interest.
- Enhancing the profession.

Each provision includes a "core principle" that outlines the reasons for and the benefits of ethical practices in public relations. The provisions also address the more substantive issues raised through the ERC research and the Ethics Board's 50 years of experience in investigating potential misconduct. Key elements of the former PRSA codes were incorporated primarily in the guidelines sections, which outline appropriate professional behavior. The guidelines, presented as affirmative, positive action statements, reflect the drafters' efforts to make the code aspirational. Explanatory statements about the "intent" of each provision, along with the careful use of the term *shall* (rather than *shall not*), also helped ensure a positive tone.

Finally, examples of "improper conduct" are provided as practical illustrations of behaviors that would violate each of the principles. The examples, particularly, were intended to expand over time, becoming "a repository for case examples of right and wrong behaviors to better and more promptly allow practitioners to determine for themselves appropriate behavior" (PRSA, 2000c, p. 26).

Code Enforcement

Perhaps the most compelling moment in BEPS deliberations was the decision on code enforcement. Research clearly showed that PRSA members and leaders supported enforcement. Yet, despite PRSA's best efforts to devise a workable code enforcement scheme, the existing process simply was not working (Fitzpatrick, 2002). In the 50 years in which the somewhat elaborate PRSA judicial system had been in effect, only 11 of 231 cases investigated had resulted in formal sanctions against members for unethical behavior. Although these statistics belie the actual work of the Ethics Board, they do reflect significant problems associated with enforcement under the former codes.

Of no small consequence was PRSA members' reluctance to get involved in enforcement proceedings (Fitzpatrick, 2002). Although required under PRSA bylaws both to report violations of fellow members and to appear as witnesses in code hearings, many members refused to participate. Additionally, many PRSA members accused of violations either resigned their membership in PRSA, thereby precluding further action by BEPS, or refused—often through their attorneys—to take part in the grievance process. Without legal subpoena power to require compliance with requests for information, the Ethics Board effectively was forced to close cases with-

out full investigations. According to BEPS legal counsel, the potential for
defamation lawsuits related to BEPS proceedings also was a concern (J. R.
Cohen, personal communication, July 3, 2001).

Notwithstanding this situation, even some BEPS members were not
convinced that eliminating code enforcement was a good idea. Of considerable concern was the potential for others to interpret a step away from
enforcement as an endorsement of unethical behavior or for PRSA members to interpret a lack of enforcement as a lack of commitment to ethics by
PRSA leaders.

> *The most significant challenge
> faced during code development
> ... was "overcoming the natural
> desire to develop a code that
> could be enforced."*

The debate on enforcement initially was framed around the issue of
whether the new code should be a punitive one with enforcement provisions, a voluntary code designed to inspire ethical conduct, or one that fell
somewhere between. Frause, who believed that code enforcement is im-
possible "without becoming a licensed profession," was a strong proponent of an aspirational and educational code. Yet he recognized the desire
for accountability. The most significant challenge faced during code development, he later recalled, was "overcoming the natural desire to develop a
code that could be enforced" (R. D. Frause, personal communication,
June 11, 2001).

ERC representatives facilitated the discussion with the earlier observa-
tion that, given the difficulties inherent in the current system, "limiting revocation of membership to cases where legal action has already taken
place would be one very conservative way of handling the problem" (ERC,
1999a, p. 10). BEPS ultimately chose this route, placing emphasis on aspirational rather than punitive elements in the new code. The decision was
based on several factors, including the lack of financial and legal resources
needed to administer a formal process of enforcement effectively, as well as
the belief that enforcement simply was not feasible without the legal authority needed to investigate fully cases of alleged misconduct.

Additionally, a review of codes of ethics adopted by nonprofit institutions and associations had produced no examples of successful enforcement mechanisms (PRSA, 2000c). In fact, it was noted that nonprofit or volunteer organizations seeking a model of an enforceable code most likely

would look to PRSA because it had one of the few codes that included a formal judicial process for punishing violators.

By targeting resources on education rather than punishment, BEPS hoped to raise public relations professionals' awareness of ethical standards and inspire them to make ethical choices. Ultimately, personal accountability was stressed through a pledge that all PRSA members—and those seeking to become members—must sign as a reflection of their commitment to the values and principles embraced by the 2000 code. The pledge states that "there is a consequence for misconduct, up to and including membership revocation" (PRSA, 2000a). Such actions are limited to "those who have been or are sanctioned by a government agency or convicted in a court of law of an action that is in violation of this Code" (PRSA, 2000a).

PRSA Approval of the New Code

Numerous drafts of the new code were discussed, debated, and rewritten in the months following the Washington meeting. In mid-2000, BEPS sent the "final" draft out for review to selected and volunteer academics and professionals in the field. Despite some concern regarding the absence of enforcement, the new code received high marks. The movement from "prohibitions" to "ideals" particularly was heralded. In the words of one draft code reviewer, "I think this positive approach to values, principles and conduct will increase the likelihood of compliance" (R. D. Frause, personal communication, July 30, 2001). Another said, "I believe the new structure of the code in terms of values, provisions and pledge, is meaningful, understandable, and helpful in furthering ethical behavior in our profession" (R. D. Frause, personal communication, July 30, 2001).

BEPS addressed the issues raised by draft reviewers and finalized the document. The next-to-last step in the process was the review and approval of the new code by the PRSA Board of Directors. With that done, BEPS requested that its proposal for a new code of ethics be placed on the agenda for the 2000 PRSA Assembly meeting. Prior to the event, the 225 Assembly delegates (who vote on behalf of chapters represented) received information about the code, along with an invitation to attend teleconferences on the subject. PRSA district chairs, chapter presidents, section chairs, and members of the College of Fellows also received information packets and invitations to participate in public forums to discuss the code proposal.

When it was formally presented on October 21, 2000, after some discussion, the proposal received resounding approval from Assembly members. The new code became effective that day, along with changes in PRSA's by-laws, which created a new role for the Ethics Board (PRSA, 2000b). Under the new system, the primary duty of BEPS is "to develop and implement educational programs regarding the Society's code of ethics for members and the public at large" (PRSA, 2000b, p. 6). BEPS also serves in an advisory role to the PRSA Board of Directors on ethics-related matters and "at the discretion and direction of the PRSA Board of Directors, as counsel to the Board" on actions related to the new code (PRSA, 2000b, p. 6).

Ethics Education

PRSA's long-term plan for its ethics education program includes establishing a staff ethics officer, volunteer chapter ethics officers and district ethics advisors; ethics programming at regional and national conferences; providing additional online ethics resources; integrating ethics-related topics in PRSA materials; sponsoring joint ethics programs with various trade groups; recognizing members' outstanding ethical practices; instituting a new member ethics orientation; establishing an ethics hot line; sponsoring Socratic dialogues, and increasing the number of forums for greater communication about ethics (PRSA, 2000c).

In the year following the code's adoption, some progress was made in weaving ethics more tightly into the fabric of PRSA and in building an internal infrastructure to support ethics initiatives. Most chapters established chapter ethics officer positions to aid chapter leaders in promoting ethics at the local level. PRSA declared February 2002 as the first annual "ethics month," during which PRSA publications featured issues related to ethics and PRSA chapters sponsored ethics programming. BEPS members discussed the establishment of a PRSA ethics advisory committee to issue formal opinions on matters related to ethics. And PRSA incorporated a link in its Web site to address members' questions and concerns about ethics issues generally and the PRSA Member Code of Ethics 2000 specifically. (See www.prsa.org.)

The Future

The 20,000 or so members of PRSA who are bound by the 2000 code represent only about one tenth of the total number of public relations practitioners in the United States. Yet, these new professional standards will have implications for practitioners in the industry as a whole, regardless of their membership status. As the leading association in the field, PRSA in many respects sets the ethical standard for the profession. As PRSA and its members gain wider recognition so, too, will the expectations for ethical performance be raised.

Additionally, questions related to professional malpractice most likely will be determined on the basis of PRSA's code of conduct. Because the

standards generally applied by the courts in such cases are based on industry norms, PRSA's guidelines most likely will provide the criteria by which
such actions will be judged.

---

*"A professional code is a living
thing which grows and improves
with the passage of time."*

In some respects, the 2000 code accomplishes a goal set by PRSA in 1993
as part of its long-range strategic plan, called "Blueprint 2000." The plan
called for PRSA to be, by the year 2000, the "standard-bearer for ethical
practice" in the industry and recognized as "the standard-setter for the
profession worldwide" (Warner, 2000, p. 15).

Of course, this will not be PRSA's last code of ethics. As the profession
and its practices evolve so, too, should the prevailing industry standards.
In fact, as the drafters of the 2000 code completed their task, they recalled
the wisdom of their early counterparts: "A professional code is a living
thing which grows and improves with the passage of time" (PRSA,
1950, p. 8.)

References

Ethics Resource Center. (1999a). *Public Relations Society of America focus group report.*
    Washington, DC: Author.
Ethics Resource Center. (1999b). *Public Relations Society of America summary report.*
    Washington, DC: Author.
Ethics Resource Center. (2000a). *Executive summary of research on ethics and profes-
    sional standards for public relations.* Washington, DC: Author.
Ethics Resource Center. (2000b.) *Public Relations Society of America survey report.*
    Washington, DC: Author.
Fitzpatrick, K. R. (2002). Evolving standards in public relations: A historical exami-
    nation of PRSA's standards of practice. *Journal of Mass Media Ethics, 17,* 89–110.
Public Relations Society of America. (1950). *Public Relations Society of America regis-
    ter.* New York: Author.
Public Relations Society of America. (2000a). *Public Relations Society of America mem-
    ber code of ethics 2000.* New York: Author.
Public Relations Society of America. (2000b). *Public Relations Society of America re-
    vised bylaws.* New York: Author.
Public Relations Society of America. (2000c). *Questions and answers about PRSA's
    new code of ethics: Briefing kit: Revising the code of ethics.* New York: Author.
Warner, H. W. (2000, January). Blueprint 2000 aims to establish public relations as a
    strategic management tool. *Public Relations Journal,* pp. 15–17.

APPENDIX
Member Code of Ethics 2000
Approved by the PRSA Assembly
October 2000

The PRSA Assembly adopted this Code of Ethics in 2000. It replaces the Code of Professional Standards (previously referred to as the Code of Ethics) that was last revised in 1988.

Preamble

Public Relations Society of America Member Code of Ethics 2000

- Professional Values
- Principles of Conduct
- Commitment and Compliance

This Code applies to PRSA members. The Code is designed to be a useful guide for PRSA members as they carry out their ethical responsibilities. This document is designed to anticipate and accommodate, by precedent, ethical challenges that may arise. The scenarios outlined in the Code provision are actual examples of misconduct. More will be added as experience with the Code occurs.

The Public Relations Society of America (PRSA) is committed to ethical practices. The level of public trust PRSA members seek, as we serve the public good, means we have taken on a special obligation to operate ethically.

The value of member reputation depends upon the ethical conduct of everyone affiliated with the Public Relations Society of America. Each of us sets an example for each other—as well as other professionals—by our pursuit of excellence with powerful standards of performance, professionalism, and ethical conduct.

Emphasis on enforcement of the Code has been eliminated. But, the PRSA Board of Directors retains the right to bar from membership or expel from the Society any individual who has been or is sanctioned by a government agency or convicted in a court of law of an action that is in violation of this Code.

Ethical practice is the most important obligation of a PRSA member. We view the Member Code of Ethics as a model for other professions, organizations, and professionals.

PRSA Member Statement of Professional Values

This statement presents the core values of PRSA members and, more broadly, of the public relations profession. These values provide the foundation for the Member Code of Ethics and set the industry standard for the professional practice of public relations. These values are the fundamental beliefs that guide our behaviors and decision-making process. We believe our professional values are vital to the integrity of the profession as a whole.

Advocacy

- We serve the public interest by acting as responsible advocates for those we represent.
- We provide a voice in the marketplace of ideas, facts, and viewpoints to aid informed public debate.

Honesty

- We adhere to the highest standards of accuracy and truth in advancing the interests of those we represent and in communicating with the public.

Expertise

- We acquire and responsibly use specialized knowledge and experience.
- We advance the profession through continued professional development, research, and education.
- We build mutual understanding, credibility, and relationships among a wide array of institutions and audiences.

Independence

- We provide objective counsel to those we represent.
- We are accountable for our actions.

Loyalty

- We are faithful to those we represent, while honoring our obligation to serve the public interest.

Fairness

- We deal fairly with clients, employers, competitors, peers, vendors, the media, and the general public.
- We respect all opinions and support the right of free expression.

PRSA Code Provisions
Free Flow of Information

Core Principle

Protecting and advancing the free flow of accurate and truthful information is essential to serving the public interest and contributing to informed decision making in a democratic society.

Intent

- To maintain the integrity of relationships with the media, government officials, and the public.
- To aid informed decision making.

Guidelines

A member shall:

- Preserve the integrity of the process of communication.
- Be honest and accurate in all communications.
- Act promptly to correct erroneous communications for which the practitioner is responsible.
- Preserve the free flow of unprejudiced information when giving or receiving gifts by ensuring that gifts are nominal, legal, and infrequent.

Examples of Improper Conduct Under This Provision:

- A member representing a ski manufacturer gives a pair of expensive racing skis to a sports magazine columnist to influence the columnist to write favorable articles about the product.
- A member entertains a government official beyond legal limits and/ or in violation of government reporting requirements.

Competition

Core Principle

Promoting healthy and fair competition among professionals preserves an ethical climate while fostering a robust business environment.

Intent

- To promote respect and fair competition among public relations professionals.
- To serve the public interest by providing the widest choice of practitioner options.

Guidelines

A member shall:

- Follow ethical hiring practices designed to respect free and open competition without deliberately undermining a competitor.
- Preserve intellectual property rights in the marketplace.

Examples of Improper Conduct Under This Provision:

- A member employed by a "client organization" shares helpful information with a counseling firm that is competing with others for the organization's business.
- A member spreads malicious and unfounded rumors about a competitor in order to alienate the competitor's clients and employees in a ploy to recruit people and business.

Disclosure of Information

Core Principle

Open communication fosters informed decision making in a democratic society.

Intent

- To build trust with the public by revealing all information needed for responsible decision making.

Guidelines

A member shall:

- Be honest and accurate in all communications.

Examples of Improper Conduct Under This Provision

- The member fails to disclose that he or she has a strong financial interest in a client's chief competitor.
- The member represents a "competitor company" or a "conflicting interest" without informing a prospective client.

Enhancing the Profession

Core Principle

Public relations professionals work constantly to strengthen the public's trust in the profession.

Intent

- To build respect and credibility with the public for the profession of public relations.
- To improve, adapt, and expand professional practices.

Guidelines

A member shall:

- Acknowledge that there is an obligation to protect and enhance the profession.
- Keep informed and educated about practices in the profession to ensure ethical conduct.
- Actively pursue personal professional development.
- Decline representation of clients or organizations that urge or require actions contrary to this Code.
- Accurately define what public relations activities can accomplish.
- Counsel subordinates in proper ethical decision making.
- Require that subordinates adhere to the ethical requirements of the Code.
- Report ethical violations, whether committed by PRSA members or not, to the appropriate authority.

Examples of Improper Conduct Under This Provision:

- A PRSA member declares publicly that a product the client sells is safe, without disclosing evidence to the contrary.
- A member initially assigns some questionable client work to a nonmember practitioner to avoid the ethical obligation of PRSA membership.

PRSA Member Code of Ethics Pledge

I pledge:

To conduct myself professionally, with truth, accuracy, fairness, and responsibility to the public; To improve my individual competence and advance the knowledge and proficiency of the profession through continuing research and education; And to adhere to the articles of the Member Code of Ethics 2000 for the practice of public relations as adopted by the governing Assembly of the Public Relations Society of America.

I understand and accept that there is a consequence for misconduct, up to and including membership revocation.

And, I understand that those who have been or are sanctioned by a government agency or convicted in a court of law of an action that is in violation of this Code may be barred from membership or expelled from the Society.

Signature:_____

Date: _____

Journal of Mass Media Ethics, 17(2), 136–154

Five Versions of One Code of Ethics: The Case Study of the Israel Broadcasting Authority

Yehiel (Hilik) Limor
Tel-Aviv University

Inés Gabel
The Open University

❏ *In this this article we trace the evolution of the Israel Broadcasting Authority's (IBA) code of ethics through 5 permutations between 1972 and 1998. We question whether the code is the outcome of a search for ethical and professional guidelines or a means of protecting the IBA from external pressures. Since 1972 the code has become more detailed, reflecting ethical, organizational, and political sensitivities. We conclude that the result of these changes has been the crystallization and implementation of normative ethical guidelines for Israeli public broadcasting.*

A popular anecdote tells of a scorpion that stood on the bank of a river and asked a frog to carry him to the opposite shore. "I'm afraid you'll sting me," answered the frog. "If I do," countered the scorpion, "we'll both drown." Persuaded by this argument, the frog allowed the scorpion to mount his back and began swimming across the river. Suddenly, he felt the sting of death. "Why did you do it?" asked the shocked frog. "It's immoral! You promised you wouldn't hurt me." "It's not a matter of morals," said the scorpion. "It's just my nature."

The story is reminiscent of media critics, some of whom blatantly declare that the media lack ethical norms (Merrill, 1991a) and exhibit amoral behavior that is implicit in their very nature because they comprise competitive organizations in a Darwinistic market economy. One particularly picturesque metaphor compares journalists to jackals (Abramson, 1991), who light on every juicy story with no concern for such basic moral issues as the right to privacy.

If journalists do behave as predators—and some say that they resemble sharks—because "neither species think about much beyond attacking and ingesting the target" (Carr, 1995)—why do so many media organizations develop codes of ethics and even try to act according to them? There are two possible explanations. First, ethics is considered to be a fundamental component of professionalism, and it can also be part of the "social responsibility" concept (Siebert, Peterson, & Schramm, 1963), whereas nonethical behavior is considered to be professionally and socially unacceptable. Second, according to the "power approach," is that ethics codes "either implicitly or explicitly, make a case against externally imposed regulations" (Allison, 1986, p. 7).

Fear of the sting that kills attacker as well as victim is a major component of the arguments propounded by supporters of media ethics codes. Without some kind of self-imposed boundaries, they claim, the media may find themselves subject to external strictures of far greater severity. The absence of moral and ethical norms is also liable to undermine the media's reliability and credibility, and thus hampers their role as "watchdogs of democracy" and as a marketplace of ideas in a democratic society.

Credibility and reliability are especially relevant and important in the case of public service broadcasting. The expectations are that public service broadcasting be impartial and that its journalists "avoid undue offence, not interject their own opinions into the debate, and in other ways serve the public interest" (Blumler, 1992, p. 13).

Public broadcasting, which exists mainly in Western Europe, but also in some other countries including Israel, has experienced a severe crisis in the last 2 decades (Tracey, 1998). As public criticism heightens, the justification for the existence of public broadcasting is being questioned and there are increased calls to abolish or privatize it. Insistence on suitable professional behavior and accountability based on ethical codes are essential to prevent further decline in the standing of public broadcasting.

The Israel Broadcasting Authority (IBA), like some other public broadcasting organizations, adopted its own ethical and professional code. This collection of guidelines, the *News Employees and Reporters' Guide* (later renamed the *News and Current Events Guide*)—and popularly nicknamed the *Nakdi Guide* after its author, veteran journalist Nakdimon Rogel—became the IBA's vade mecum for matters of ethics and professional standards. First published in 1972, it has been updated four times: in 1979, 1985, 1995, and most recently in 1998. The original version had 42 sections, whereas the most recent one has 169—a fourfold increase.[1] This article traces the motives for formulating IBA's code of ethics and for its recurrent revision. The main question is as follows: Is the code the outcome of a search for ethical and professional guidelines, or does it serve other aims, mainly to protect the IBA from external pressures?

Such research is of interest not only as a historical study of IBA's development or of journalistic ethics in general, but also of the existential struggle of public broadcasting at a time when both the concept and the very existence of public broadcasting are being challenged.

Levels of Media Accountability

Codes of ethics are just one mechanism among media accountability systems (Bertrand, 2000). We can define five levels of media accountability—two statutory and three voluntary—some or all of which are in force in most democratic countries. The two statutory levels are basic laws and secondary legislation, and the three voluntary levels are the institutional level, the medium level, and the organizational level (Limor, 2002).

The first and most binding level of media accountability is statutory, wherein the internal supervision systems of the media institution are derived from basic laws and draw their power from them. Various free professions, especially medicine, law, psychology, and social work, operate within a statutory framework that accords them not only social legitimacy but also legal recognition. One characteristic of such professions is a code of ethics, with internal systems to supervise adherence to the code, punish violators, and in extreme cases, even ban offenders from the profession. Examples of countries with such media legislation are India, in which the Press Council operates by virtue of the 1965 Press Council Act (Trikha, 1986), and Denmark, in which the Code of Conduct is part of the 1992 Media Liability Act (Kruuse, 1994; Laitila, 1995).

Media accountability systems of secondary legislation are not anchored directly in legislation. Nevertheless, the law authorizes (and sometimes even compels) certain bodies to institute codes of ethics that are granted statutory validity. Examples prevailing in the United Kingdom include the Code of Practice of the Broadcasting Standards Council and the regulations determined by the Independent Television Commission and the Radio Authority.

Accountability systems on the institutional level address the media institution as a whole. The most salient example is the press council common to all mass media, both print and electronic. Such councils are active in various countries, including Belgium, Denmark, the Netherlands, Turkey, Finland, and others (Sonninen & Laitila, 1995), as well as in the state of Minnesota (News Council). The Israel Press Council (IPC), which is considered the highest representative of the Israeli media (Caspi & Limor, 1999), can be included in this category, although in fact it covers mostly the print media.

Single medium-level systems are operated by the organizations of a single medium. Outstanding examples include the British Press Complaints Commission that covers only the print media and the Press Councils of Sweden, Norway, and Germany. Other examples are the Statement of Principles of the Association of Newspaper Editors (ASNE), and the codes of ethics of the Society of Professional Journalists, and the National Press Photographers Association.

The organizational level applies to two types of organizations, those operating by force of law (primarily public broadcasting systems) and privately owned media organizations. Examples of the first type include the *BBC Producers' Guidelines* and the *Journalistic Standards and Practices* of the Canadian Broadcasting Authority. Examples of the second type are internal guidelines by individual newspapers (such as the *New York Times' Guidelines on Our Integrity* or the *Washington Post's Standard and Ethics*), newspaper chains (such as *Gannett's Principle of Ethical Conduct for Newsrooms* or *Scripps' Statement of Policy on Ethics and Professional Conduct*) or news agencies (such *as Reuters' Handbook for Journalists* or the *Associated Press Stylebook and Libel Manual*), although some of these combine ethics directives and professional code of conduct. Ombudsmen maintained by many newspapers in the United States, Canada, Brazil, Japan, Spain, and elsewhere belong to this category as well.

The *Nakdi Guide* is anchored in the organizational level, although law established the IBA itself. One should note that all other electronic media in Israel have codes of ethics that are anchored in the secondary legislation level, which are the *Ethics Regulations* of the Second Authority for Television and Radio and of the Cable Television Broadcasting Council.[2] All codes have effectively adopted many of the standard ethical principles of Western media, including objectivity and fairness in broadcasting, right of response, nondisclosure of sources of information, and so on.

The *Nakdi Guide* serves as a kind of internal substitute for the Code of Ethics of the IPC, to which the IBA does not belong. In fact, many of the ethical principles determined by the IPC were adopted post facto by the IBA and included in the *Nakdi Guide* (Limor & Gabel, 1999). Many of IBA's employees are effectively subject to the IPC's authority by virtue of their membership in the National Federation of Israeli Journalists, one of the IPC's component bodies.[3] There were cases in which the IBA barred its employees from appearing before the IPC's ethics courts even when complaints were lodged against them, stating that IBA employees are legally subject to the IBA's own disciplinary court, which enjoys the same legal authority as civil service disciplinary courts. Consequently, they are not to be rendered liable to possible double jeopardy.

Codes of Ethics: Two Approaches

Adopting a code of ethics, which can be viewed as a professional "conscience" (Allison, 1986), is one of the main characteristics of any profession. Therefore, any attempt to discuss codes of ethics should be done within the broader framework of professionalism. Two contradictory approaches to professionalism exist, both relevant to the IBA case.

The first approach, the structural–functional approach, tries to define a profession according to certain criteria. Classical studies (Cullen, 1978; Hall,

1968) identify a series of criteria such as systematic and theoretical body of knowledge, formal education, social recognition, and service to the public.

One claim is that codes of ethics and the ideal of service are mere rhetoric that assist in the preservation of power and the principal criterion for defining a profession (Moore, 1970); others believe that the formal and informal professional cultures distinguish a profession from other occupations (Greenwood, 1957). Freidson (1994) used the term *profession* to refer to "an occupation that controls its own work, organized by a special set of institutions sustained in part by a particular ideology of expertise and service" (p. 10).

The critical approach to professionalism views professions as monopolistic occupations that use codes of ethics as a tool to preserve their exclusive social status and privileges. The claim is that codes of ethics and the ideal of service are mere rhetoric that assists in the preservation of power and autonomy, or in Ladinsky's (1981) words, "Public claims of self-control and devotion to service are delusions used to pacify and confuse the public and clients" (p. 5).

Although journalists and media personnel agree that ethical principals are important to their profession—which is partially proved by the fact that hundreds of media and journalists' organizations adopted codes of ethics—the codes themselves are controversial (Day, 2000). Widespread criticism of codes of ethics includes statements such as the following: codes are "largely an exercise in public relations" (Brennan, 1996, p. 114); very few journalists rely on codes when they confront ethical dilemmas (Fink, 1995); whether codes establish the lower or the upper level of ethical behavior is unclear (Reuss, 1996). Others claim that codes impede libertarian and individualistic philosophy (Merrill, 1974) or that "codes may well be founded on a non-ethical basis, and thus may lead to non-ethical behavior" (Black & Barney, 1985, p. 30). And, of course, the main criticism, which is heard repeatedly from researchers as well as from media workers, is the lack of enforcement. Criticizing codes of ethics is not unique to journalism. Criticism of codes and their efficiency is common to other professions, such as engineering (Davis, 1991).

At least some of the criticism of ethical codes may not be relevant to the IBA or other public broadcasting organizations because these bodies, especially if they are established by law, have enforcement mechanisms in the form of internal disciplinary tribunals, which are authorized to judge a journalist who exhibits unprofessional or unethical behavior.

Public Broadcasting in the New Era

Since the earliest days of broadcasting, "discussions, debates and even battles have been waged" (Limburg, 1994, p. 9) over the question of whether qualitative standards ought to be set for broadcasting. Even when the National Association of Broadcasters (NAB) adopted its Statement of Principles of Radio and TV in 1990, broadcasters felt that "it should be the receivers [listeners and viewers] who determined the ethics of what they chose to receive, rather than the senders [broadcasters]" (Limburg, 1994, p. 9).

Their colleagues in Europe did not enter into the ethics debate of U.S. broadcasters. In the United States, broadcasting developed as an economic enterprise (notwithstanding federal supervision) from the outset, beginning with radio and then television. In Europe, however, the broadcasting media were largely state owned and controlled by the government; their ethical norms, even if not always stipulated in writing, effectively reflected prevailing political conceptions and the values and norms that the government sought to instill in the general public. Only when the broadcasting media were separated from the government and became public–state broadcasting authorities did they have to address the ethical–professional issues that concerned their colleagues throughout the world, in the print media and electronic media alike. In Europe and elsewhere, the development of commercial broadcasting over the past few decades—paralleling that of public broadcasting—gave rise to a multifaceted crisis for the latter.

One aspect of this crisis is structural in nature; namely, shattering a monopoly (Rolland & Ostbye, 1986), bringing public broadcasting face to face with new, privately held broadcasting channels. The second aspect is economic: The public media, as complex bureaucratic bodies dependent primarily on licensing fees for their income, found competing with the economic power of private broadcasting organizations difficult. Inflationary maelstroms and a government policy of avoiding drastic rises in license fees further weakened the financial capabilities of public broadcasting (Richeri, 1986). A third facet, perhaps the most important of all, is identity: The new commercial broadcasting channels forced public broadcasting to shape a unique identity, differentiating it from private, commercial broadcasting organizations. After all, if no difference exists in outlook, function, and content between public and commercial radio and television stations, why should public broadcasting be entitled to collect license fees, which in fact amount to indirect taxation, from the general public? On the other hand, not attempting to respond to public needs and tastes could lead to a sharp decline in ratings, again arousing public and political demand for cancellation of licensing fees.

Over the past few years, we have witnessed various attempts to characterize public broadcasting and shape its special identity profile. Such endeavors were launched in the United Kingdom (Blumler, 1992; BRU, 1986), for example, whose public broadcasting system (the British Broadcasting Company, or BBC) was the archetype of public broadcasting authorities in Europe and elsewhere, including Israel (Caspi & Limor, 1999), and in Israel

(Ezrahi Ben-Shachar & Lahl, 1997). All such suggested identity profiles, either overtly or implied, also entail the need for a code of ethics to guide public broadcasting organizations and personnel who face a key dilemma: Should they behave in the same manner (including ethics) as their colleagues in the privately owned media or are they bound by other behavioral rules?

The *Nakdi Guide*: Five Incarnations

The first version of the *Nakdi Guide* explicitly stated that its purpose was to emphasize and clarify several of the professional injunctions that exemplify the function of radio and television news personnel insofar as the nature of the medium is concerned (paralleling the print media), as well as that of the IBA as a public–state broadcasting organization that operates by virtue of law (Rogel, 1972). Indeed, the guide has two components: a code of ethics and a professional guidebook. In addition to providing comprehensive definitions of ethical guidelines, it also addresses the practical issues deriving from these definitions. In this respect, it resembles the guides formulated by major broadcasting media to govern their activities, such as the BBC's *Producers' Guidelines* or the Canadian Broadcasting Corporation's *Journalistic Standards and Practices*.

Codes of ethics are customarily compendia of noncompulsory advice or injunction-free behavioral guidelines (Pasqua, 1990). The *Nakdi Guide* is more comprehensive. It not only stipulates explicit dos and don'ts, but also incorporates legal directives, ethical rules common to all media, statutory prohibitions, and intraorganizational guidelines that conform to the nature of the electronic media in general and the IBA's status as a public–state authority in particular. Moreover, transgressions against the guide's instructions can end up in a disciplinary court.

Why did the IBA need the *Nakdi Guide*? The three possible explanations are ethical–professional, organizational, and political.

Ethical–Professional

The Broadcasting Authority Law (1965) stipulated that the IBA must ensure that its broadcasts "reflect the appropriate expression of different outlooks and opinions prevailing among the public and transmit reliable information" (Section 4). The fledgling authority was thus charged with tackling professional issues that concern the entire journalism profession. Such issues are indeed addressed in ethical guidelines, such as the IPC's Code of Ethics. Because the IBA was subject to the terms of the Broadcasting Authority Law and to the supervision of the State Comptroller, it could not adopt the IPC's Code of Ethics, but rather had to formulate its own, including features unique to public broadcasting.

Organizational

In 1965, 7 years before the original version of the *Nakdi Guide* was published, the Broadcasting Authority Law was passed, transforming Israel Radio (Kol Israel) from a government department in the Prime Minister's Office to an independent public–state broadcasting authority. When Israel Television was established in 1968 and incorporated into the IBA, the law was applied to it as well. In 1972 the IBA was still in the early stages of its consolidation as an independent authority, and the new organizational framework demanded work regulations adapted to changing realities, including clarification of the status and function of journalists, who had previously been government employees and now became employees of an independent authority. The importance of these regulations increased for three additional reasons: (a) the inclusion of a new medium, television, whose work patterns differed from that of the old and familiar medium of radio; (b) expansion of the organization by adding new channels within the IBA; and (c) changes on the media map (when the IBA's monopoly was broken by the creation of new commercial competitors, both in radio and television) engendering the need to determine organizational norms.

Political

Although the political establishment accorded the IBA its independence, politicians were unwilling to relinquish their control over broadcasting channels quite so easily. The political establishment perceived the IBA as an instrument of the government and not as the public–state instrument that the law mandated. In effect, the greater the independence displayed by the IBA, the greater the criticism by the political establishment, which did not hesitate to intervene, directly and indirectly, in IBA functions (Caspi & Limor, 1999).

Tension between the political establishment and a public–state broadcasting authority is not unique to Israel. A similar picture emerges in Western Europe (Richeri, 1986) and in Australia, as Quentin Dempster of the Australian Broadcasting Authority (ABA) indicated: "None of our leaders has accepted as legitimate the mildly inquisitive, sometimes provocative and mainstream public broadcasting system" (Australian Center for Independent Journalism, 1996).

The tense relations between the political establishment and the young IBA peaked in 1972 and may have been the chief catalyst for compiling of the *Nakdi Guide* and for IBA's adopting it. As the guide's author attested,

> The Government is not yet accustomed to an independent broadcasting authority. The Executive Committee sought to appoint a "commissar" in charge

of news alongside the Director-General. The Director-General objected and proposed compiling a behavioral code as an alternative. I was charged with that mission. (Shalit, 1995, p. 32)

Formulating the *Nakdi Guide* and ethical principles was thus IBA's deliberate attempt to develop the means to halt external pressure. Effectively, the IBA had to adopt the rationale for establishing press councils in many Western countries and for their codes of ethics (i.e., the introduction of internal supervision to prevent imposition of external control). Indeed, an examination of 31 codes of ethics of journalists' associations in Europe indicates that one key function of these regulations is to protect the professional integrity of journalists faced with external pressures (Laitila, 1995).

All three explanations—the ethical–professional, the organizational, and the political—are relevant to the revisions of the *Nakdi Guide*. Since its first version in 1972, considerable changes have taken place in Israel's political and social atmosphere and in its broadcasting bodies. The IBA lost its monopoly with the establishment of commercial channels[4]—a new commercial television channel, cable television channels, and local radio stations operated by private franchisees. These developments placed the IBA in a position of fierce competition that weakened its professional and ethical norms. Under these circumstances, the IBA was compelled to formulate new professional and ethical principles and to ensure their enforcement. In his introduction to the most recent version of the *Nakdi Guide*, the IBA's director-general hints at the need to cope with the new situation: "In recent years, perhaps because of bitter commercial competition, there has been a weakening in the enforcement of the rules" (Rogel, 1998, p. 9). The fact that the IPC had its own code of ethics and revised it periodically also pressured IBA to ensure the *Nakdi Guide* remained up-to-date. The political upheavals and the frequent changes in governments, rather than lessening the political pressure on the IBA, increased it. In addition, social developments such as the consolidation of ethnic subcultures compelled the IBA to review its ethical/professional and organizational norms.

The original version of the *Nakdi Guide*, published in 1972, had 42 sections; 7 years later, in 1979, a short time after a new IBA director-general was appointed, Rogel was asked to update the guide and adapt it to changing circumstances. This was one reflection of the change of government in Israel: In 1977 the right-wing Likud Party assumed power, having defeated the Labor Party that had ruled the country since its establishment in 1948. The new director-general was identified with right-wing views and his appointment signified the new government's decision to restrain the IBA, whose independent activity was perceived by the right as identified with liberal and leftist views. The update yielded an expanded *Nakdi Guide* with 72 sections (Rogel, 1979). In 1985, when a left–right coalition was in power, the *Nakdi Guide* was revised once again. The number of sections was reduced by one, but the number of topics covered increased considerably (Rogel, 1985). In 1995, after Labor again took the helm, the director-general (identified with the left-wing government that had appointed him) again ordered that the *Nakdi Guide* be revised. This edition swelled to 161 sections (Rogel & Schejter, 1995). The Labor government held on for less than 4 years. When the 1996 elections brought the right back to power, a new director-general with right-wing affiliations was appointed, who ordered yet another revision of the *Nakdi Guide*. The latest edition, published in 1998, has 169 sections (Rogel, 1998).

Although the IBA perceives the *Nakdi Guide* as a binding handbook, its institutions avoided anchoring it in legally binding regulations. Consequently, the *Nakdi Guide* has remained an aggregate of intraorganizational guidelines of lesser legal status than the codes of ethics of other broadcasting media in Israel, such as the Second Authority for Television and Radio.[5]

The *Nakdi Guide:* Changes Over the Years

Differences among editions of the *Nakdi Guide* can be assessed according to two parameters: (a) the number of new sections in each edition, and (b) the number of amendments and additions to existing sections. Content analysis of the *Nakdi Guide*'s various editions, according to the three factors that explain its creation and its changes—ethical–professional, organizational, and political—shows that the lines between the factors are frequently blurred. A section (or amendment) can, for example, serve organizational goals while adopting ethical norms and establishing a political-proof shield.

The category addressed by the greatest number of new sections and amendments is that of ethical–professional guidelines. For example, in 1979, the following guidelines were added to the *Nakdi Guide:* "Erroneous items are to be corrected at the earliest opportunity" (Rogel, 1979, Section 32), and "The user of a source of information [who is unwilling to be identified] must protect that source's anonymity" (Section 34). In 1985 a new section determined limitations and professional guidelines for coverage of the stock market and economic affairs (Rogel, 1985, Section 16b).[6] The 1995 edition had the largest and most significant number of new sections added in this sphere: 61 amendments and additions. These amendments include issues such as preventing demonstrators or demonstration organizers from using the broadcaster's microphone to transmit appeals to the public to join said demonstration (Rogel & Schejter, 1995, Section 104); directions on "ambushing interviewees" (Section 79); caution in disclosing the name of a person suspected of violence (Section 125); and restrictions on filming funerals contrary to the wishes of the deceased's family (Section 116).

In 1985 a section concerning guidelines on reporting terrorist attacks and public order disturbances was added. Among other things it determined that reports should "be based solely on facts in the field and avoid descriptions of impressions" (Section 59). The 1985 edition also stipulated that if the police refuse to submit an estimate of the number of participants in a demonstration, one might refer to it as "small, large or mass" (Section 50). Another new section (Section 51a) indicates that "IBA personnel ought not use value-laden adjectives in referring to labor disputes," and still another section clarified that "a reporter or photographer is disqualified from covering an issue in which he is personally involved or whose personal interests could be affected by the article's outcome" (Section 16a). The 1995 version includes new instructions such as "Household appliances and other items should not be called by popular trade names" (Section 154).

The second category—the organizational—is mainly reflected in amendments and additions targeted to strengthen the management's control and supervision. Content analysis of the *Nakdi Guide,* in its various manifestations, points to an increasing tendency toward IBA centralization, entailing approval by the highest echelons for more and more media activities.[7] Although the original version only had three sections stipulating that certain activities require the director-general's approval, the most recent edition (Rogel, 1998) lists 21 such cases. The director-general holds the highest management position in the IBA and is responsible for four media directors (Hebrew Television, Arabic Television, Hebrew Radio, and Arabic Radio), subordinate to each of whom are division directors (including the News Division) and department directors of the respective media. This increase in the director-general' powers has been accompanied by an increase—although somewhat less marked—in the extent of centrality among media directors and a decline (or at least stagnation) in authority delegated to lower echelons (e.g., division or department directors, editors). One should note that five of the seven directors-general serving the IBA between 1965 and 1998 sought to leave their personal mark in this field by formulating or amending a code of ethics.

Centralization is reflected most prominently in the numerous sections added in the later editions, especially those in 1995 and 1998, stipulating activities requiring approval by or advance consultation with senior executives. These restrictions have both intraorganizational and extraorganizational implications. Within the organization, they are likely to ensure uniformity and preservation of professional norms, as well as institutionalization of a rigid and clearly defined structural hierarchy. On the other hand, they are liable to weaken the autonomy of the lower echelons and even the development of self-sufficiency skills among individual journalists. Outside the IBA, intensification of centralization may block pressure because it embodies a kind of proof of the presence of a "boss" who bears responsibility and is the obvious target for complaints.

The changes and amendments in the third category—the political—reflect changes in power on the political map. Some conspicuous examples are the following: In 1979 a clarification was added indicating that the political background of the commentator should be mentioned when his political beliefs pertain to the issue under discussion. The 1985 edition addressed the issue of coverage of the Territories and the PLO for the first time. It stipulates that the terms *Judea* and *Samaria* should be used to designate areas under Israeli control and not the *West Bank*—"except when quoting others directly." It also determined that one should not refer to the "Palestinian flag" but rather the "PLO (Palestine Liberation Organization) flag." In that same edition, to ensure that the IBA does not serve as a platform for propaganda by "elements that are overtly hostile to the State of Israel and fight against it (and the PLO is such an element)," the IBA director-general, by decision of the Executive Committee, is charged with "reviewing every interview conducted in Judea and Samaria and the Gaza District" and determining which may be broadcast. In contrast, the edition published in 1995 (after the signing of the Oslo Agreements between Israel and the Palestinians) states that interviews with Palestinian leaders are considered the same as other interviews. In this version, Palestinian leaders are called "personalities," whereas 10 years earlier, the *Nakdi Guide* included a veiled directive not to call PLO leaders "personalities" because of the positive connotation of respect and importance inherent in that term.

A new section in 1995 determined that "the IBA does not rule out the broadcasting of opinions and outlooks of any type whatsoever."[8] In the same edition, the following instruction was added: "There is no city called 'East Jerusalem.'"[9]

Another issue that can be partially defined as political is the coverage of terrorism and security topics. This issue was first addressed in 1979. The additions emphasized that in reporting terrorist acts, one should avoid "excessive horror" and "maintain as factually-oriented a tone as possible" (Section 59). The 1985 edition stipulated that one should not broadcast news of the number of enemy casualties based on enemy sources alone (Section 62a). In 1995 guidelines were added regarding use of terms such as *slaughter, massacre, murderous attack,* and the like (Section 72).

Reasons for the Additions and Revisions

Day (2000) claimed that "ethical decisions are always made within a specific context, which includes the political, social, and cultural climate" (p. 5). Ethical decisions depend on time and circumstances, as do the ethical codes consolidating the normative framework in which such decisions are made. Indeed, journalistic ethics are not only exclusively a product of the profession but also of social conceptions regarding the media's role in a society operating according to given behavioral and ideological codes. In the case of the *Nakdi Guide*, the changes not only reflect purely ethical–professional needs—themselves the result of changes and developments (such as competition) on the media map—but also are perhaps primarily a reflection of changes in the political, social, and cultural conditions within which the IBA operates.

The various changes address three distinct but interrelated spheres of activity. The outermost sphere is sociocultural, the second sphere includes the media institution, and the third and innermost sphere represents the IBA.

The outermost sphere includes other social institutions, as well as pressure and interest groups. The IBA's status as a public–state authority enjoying a long-term monopoly in news and current affairs broadcasting naturally intensified attempts at supervision and exertion of influence. Such pressure is particularly evident in three areas of activity—political, social, and religious—each of which reflects a rift in Israeli society.

Since the 1967 Six-Day War in which the West Bank (including East Jerusalem) was occupied, Israeli society has been polarized between those who oppose withdrawal from the West Bank and its cession to the Palestinians, claiming that the Territories are part of the Land of Israel and are essential to security, and those who perceive withdrawal as a vital step toward achieving peace in the Middle East, oppose ruling the Palestinian people and recognize its right to an independent state. This political schism, which culminated in the 1995 assassination of Prime Minister Yitzhak Rabin by a right-wing extremist, affects all aspects of life in Israel and gives rise to constant pressure on the IBA regarding coverage of political and social issues, as well as criticism of content and even terminology from right-wing and left-wing circles alike.

Parallel to the right–left political rift, the social gap between religious (especially the ultraorthodox) and secular Jews in Israel has sharply intensified, especially over the past 5 years. The religious and ultraorthodox sector has gradually accumulated political power—deriving from the inability of the major political parties, right and left alike, to gain a parliamentary majority and their consequent solicitation of religious parties for participation in coalitions—and used it in an attempt to influence broadcast content and work patterns at the IBA. Although the number of *Nakdi Guide* sections directly concerned with religious issues is relatively small, journalists fearing that pressure from the religious–political establishment may curtail their initiatives are liable to justify their behavior by resorting to the *Nakdi Guide* as an excuse or protective umbrella to protect the traditional framework of the IBA, which reflects a civil, secular, and democratic culture.

The middle sphere represents the media institution, primarily comprising dozens or even hundreds of media organizations. This institution influences the IBA in two respects—normative and practical. The primary normative influence originates in the IPC perceived as the supreme body of the media institution in Israel (Caspi & Limor, 1999). Its decisions concerning professional ethics affect the IBA and have numerous direct and indirect manifestations on the *Nakdi Guide,* just as they affect ethical regulations determined by the Second Authority for Television and Radio and the Cable Television Broadcasting Council. In the practical sphere, the influence of interaction and competition with other media organizations, both print and electronic, is highly evident, as the professional norms, work patterns, and output of a given medium or media organization also trickle down to other media organizations.

The third and innermost sphere is the IBA itself. Two secondary circles may be discerned within it, the first consisting of public bodies legally responsible for IBA administration and the second comprising IBA's journalists. Positions in public bodies are filled according to political and party criteria that may even be overtly declared. Party representatives in these bodies attempt to impose supervision of routine IBA operation, according an internal manifestation to political, social, and religious pressures applied on the IBA in any case. In the second inner circle, the journalists constantly strive for professional autonomy such as that of their print media colleagues in the spirit of the conception of social responsibility that gradually displaced the mobilized media or development media models.

Establishing the IBA as a public–state body in 1965 was supposed to liberate it from the political establishment's stranglehold and government control and propel it toward the social responsibility model (i.e., self-supervision of the media entailing professional autonomy). More than 35 years have passed since that time, but the IBA still has not achieved autonomous, pressure-free broadcasting in the spirit of social responsibility.

The pace of transition from the government-supervised broadcasting pattern to autonomy has been affected by a series of cross-pressures that alternately propel the IBA forward (positive pressure) or block and sometimes retard its progress (negative pressure). Positive pressures include social processes of democratization that also affect the status and role of the media, particularly regarding legitimization of its function as the "watchdog of Democracy." Fierce competition among the various media, which encourages the slaughter of journalism's sacred cows, compels public broadcasting to cope with changing realities by reconciling itself to and internalizing new norms or simply as a means of survival in an attempt to position itself versus the private and commercial media.

Pressures that block progress toward the social responsibility model originate primarily in the political institution that is not willing to relinquish the reins of tight IBA control. Politicians perceive television and radio as an effective tool for marketing hegemony and ideology and personal promotion, especially in an age of party primaries. Other institutions, each in its own way, try to limit the IBA and influence its activity. Moreover, various pressure groups try to check IBA autonomy; some seek to impose control of various types, including supervision of programming patterns, content, and even broadcasts themselves. Pressures initiated by the religious institution, which sometimes even lead to informal censorship (Limor & Nossek, 2000), are just one example. Political appointments to the public bodies overseeing the IBA and especially to the director-general's post help ensure the conforming to prevailing ideology, intensifying centralization, checking progress toward the social responsibility pole, or a combination thereof.

Conclusions

Two principal reasons exist for the formulation of the *Nakdi Guide* in 1972 and its adoption by the IBA. The first and most important was the attempt to create a "shield" against external pressures, especially those applied by the political establishment. The second was the need for a binding system of professional regulations aimed at achieving professionalism and uniformity in the developing organization's work procedures, as well as clarifying its hierarchical authority and decision-making structure. The outcome of all pressures, extraorganizational and intraorganizational, was the formulation of a code of ethics.

The pressures and constraints that gave rise to the first edition of the *Nakdi Guide* did not lose intensity over the years; in fact, some even intensified. Cross-pressures from without and within compelled the IBA to update the *Nakdi Guide* periodically, expanding it and adapting it to changing political, societal, and professional realities. As such, the *Nakdi Guide* served and still serves a dual purpose, preserving conventional organizational and professional–ethical norms while responding, if only partially, to dynamic circumstances mainly in the political sphere. Such revisions also constitute an attempt to cope with the situation Richard Cunningham (1988) described, "It can be frightening for journalists and others to sail on a boundless sea without traditional anchors" (p. 16).

As indicated, a code of ethics should also serve as a means of internal supervision to prevent imposition of external control and adverse effects on professional autonomy. The greater the external pressures for control of the media, the greater the need for expansion of the code of ethics. The IBA code thus not only drills staff in the dos and don'ts of the profession but also proves to external forces (e.g., political, social) that the IBA is a credible body with a comprehensive and rigid system of accountability and self-regulation.

Black and Barney (1985) claimed that, "The strength of a[n] ethical code is a function not only of its various canons, but of its legitimacy and power in the eyes for whom it is written" (p. 31). The question is, for whom was the *Nakdi Guide* written? Was it written for the journalists working in the organization, and thus aimed to function as a sort of a written course in ethics and organizational norms, or was it written for politicians, in an attempt to convince them that the IBA is capable of self-regulation, and thereby negating the need for external (i.e., political) control? The answer in this case is clear, as evidenced by the guide's author. Paradoxically, although the guide was originally designed as a shield against political control, it became over the years the deontological code of ethics of the IBA and was even adopted, formally or informally, by other broadcasting organizations. Ethical concerns are not always the original motives and reasons for formulating codes of ethics, yet, the result—at least in the case of IBA—was the crystallization of normative ethical guidelines and their implementation. In other words, even if the *Nakdi Guide* was founded on a nonethical basis, in practice it led to ethical behavior.

On the other hand, the proliferation of new sections in the *Nakdi Guide* may lead IBA staff to refrain from adopting it or following its behavioral guidelines. Former *Los Angeles Times* editor William Thomas, quoted by John Merrill (1991b), summed up the situation thusly: "I've never seen a written code of ethics that wasn't so damned obvious that it was clear that you were doing it more for its outside PR value than for any inward impact" (p. 163).

Notes

1. The first three editions of the *Nakdi Guide* were mimeographed and distributed only among IBA employees, whereas the fourth edition was hardbound and offered for sale to the general public (Rogel & Schejter, 1995). The most recent edition (Rogel, 1998) was published in a booklet format and distributed only among IBA employees.
2. The High Court of Justice rejected an appeal demanding that the IBA render the *Nakdi Guide* obligatory with legal status resembling that of the Second Authority for Television and Radio and Cable Television Broadcasting Council Codes of Ethics. In its decision, the court concurred with the IBA, declaring that it is not obliged to change the document's status (High Court of Justice, Docket No. 3504/96).
3. The other two components are the daily newspaper owners and editors, and representatives of the public. The IPC's president and his deputy are public representatives.
4. Cable television was introduced in Israel in the late 1980s; the Second (commercial) television channel was introduced in 1993; local (commercial) radio stations were introduced in the 1990s. Although cable television and local radio stations do not produce news, the Second television channel broadcasts news programs and competes with the first (public service) channel.

5. Section 33 of the Broadcasting Authority Law empowers the IBA Executive Committee to determine regulations that have statutory validity with the approval of the relevant Cabinet Minister. However, the IBA refrained from rendering the entire *Nakdi Guide* legally binding. The only exception is the "IBA Regulations (provision of opportunity for response to an injured party) 1997," which accord legal status to ethical rules calling for soliciting an advance reaction from people liable to be adversely affected by an impending broadcast and subsequently transmitting their reactions.

6. The additions to the *Nakdi Guide* effectively reflect an IPC guideline issued 6 years earlier, determining rules for press coverage of the stock exchange. Other sections added over the years also reflect IPC decisions, such as those concerning interviews with minors or close-ups of mourners.

7. Some conspicuous examples are the following: The original 1972 version prohibited "concealed recording and/or photographic equipment in news and current affairs offices ... except with the approval of the Director-General or anyone in whom he vests authority" (Section 28), whereas in the next version (1979) the instruction was amended as follows: "except with the approval of the Director-General or the Legal Advisor" (Section 45). In the 1985 version the following instruction was added: "No laws should be broken, even ostensibly so, for any purpose whatsoever in the course of preparing an item except with the approval of the IBA Legal Advisor" (Section 48). The 1995 edition states that "polls conducted by telephone to the studio while on the air, in pro-or-con format, are permitted only with the approval of the Media Director" (section 56), and the 1998 edition declares that such surveys are permissible "only with the approval of the Director-General" (Section 53).

8. This section anchors the IBA guideline issued following the ruling by the High Court of Justice on a petition submitted by extreme right-wing Knesset member Rabbi Meir Kahane (High Court of Justice, Docket No. 399/85), who appealed to the court after the IBA imposed severe restrictions on broadcasting interviews with him, quoting his verbal manifestos and news and articles concerning his activities. The court determined that the restrictions were unjustified and constituted discrimination.

9. Israel captured East Jerusalem, formerly under Jordanian rule, in the 1967 Six-Day War. Although in everyday parlance Israelis use the expression "East Jerusalem" to refer to the area largely populated by Arabs, right-wing circles demanded that the public–state broadcasting media avoid using that expression because it ostensibly hints at the existence of two separate cities.

References

Abramson, J. (1991). Four criticisms of press ethics. In J. Lichtenberg (Ed.), *Democracy and the mass media* (pp. 229–268). Cambridge, England: Cambridge University Press.

Allison, M. (1986). A literature review of approaches to the professionalism of journalists. *Journal of Mass Media Ethics, 1,* 5–19.

Australian Center for Independent Journalism. (1996). *The crisis in Australian public broadcasting.* Sydney: University of Technology. Retrieved August 31, 2001 from http://acij.uts.edu.au/old_acij/ACIJ/Crisis/crisis.html

Bertrand, C. J. (2000). *Media ethics and accountability systems.* New Brunswick, NJ: Transaction.

Black, J., & Barney, R. (1985). The case against mass media codes of ethics. *Journal of Mass Media Ethics, 1,* 27–36.

Blumler, J. (1992). Public service broadcasting before the commercial deluge. In J. Blumler (Ed.), *Television and the public interest* (pp. 7–21). London: Sage.

Brennan, B. (1996). Codes of ethics: Who needs them? In V. Alia, B. Brennan, & B. Hoffmaster (Eds.), *Deadlines and diversity: Journalism ethics in a changing world* (pp. 112–120). Halifax, Nova Scotia: Fernwood.

Broadcasting Research Unit. (1986). *The public service idea in British broadcasting.* London: Author.

Carr, D. (1995). Journalists: Sharks with a conscience. Retrieved April 25, 1998 from Minnesota News Council's Web site, http://www.mtn.org/~newscncl/ spring95/Carr.html

Caspi, D., & Limor, Y. (1999). *The in/outsiders: The media in Israel.* Cresskill, NJ: Hampton Press.

Cullen, J. (1978). *The structure of professionalism.* New York: Petrocelli.

Cunningham, R. (1988, November). The press as a moral arbiter. *The Quill,* p. 16.

Davis, M. (1991). Thinking like an engineer: The place of a code of ethics in the practice of a profession. *Philosophy & Public Affairs, 20,* 150–167.

Day, L. (2000). *Ethics in media communications: Cases and controversies* (3rd ed.). Belmont, CA: Wadsworth.

Ezrahi, Y. (1997). *Reforma Ba-Shidur Ha-Tziburi* [Reform in the public broadcasting]. Jerusalem: Israeli Democracy Institute (Position Paper No. 1).

Fink, C. (1995). *Media ethics.* Boston: Allyn & Bacon.

Freidson, E. (1994). *Professionalism reborn: Theory, prophecy and policy.* Chicago: University of Chicago Press.

Greenwood, E. (1957). Attributes to professions. *Social Work, 2,* 45–55.

Hall, R. (1968). Professionalization and bureaucratization. *American Sociological Review, 33,* 92–104.

Kruuse, H. N. (1994). Press ethics in Denmark. In H. Kruuse, M. Berlins, & C. Grellier, (Eds.), *Les droits et les devoirs des journalistes dans les douz pays de l'Union Europeenne.* Paris: Centre de Formation et de Perfectionment des Journalists. Retrieved September 27, 1997 from http:/www.djh.dk/personale/ helle_nissen_kruuse/Press%20Ethics.dk.html

Ladinsky, J. (1981). The professions. In M. Smith & A. Wertheimer (Eds.), *Pharmacy practice: Social and behavioral aspects* (pp. 1–11). New York: Williams & Wilkins.

Laitila, T. (1995). Journalistic codes of ethics in Europe. *European Journal of Communication, 10,* 527–544.

Limburg, V. (1994). *Electronic media ethics.* Boston: Focal Press.

Limor, Y. (2002). Media accountability systems in Israel: You'll never know it's there. In C. J. Bertrand (Ed.), *An arsenal for democracy: Media accountability systems* (pp. 379–392). Cresskill, NJ: Hampton Press.

Limor, Y., & Gabel, I. (1999, August). *Conservation vs. dynamism: Five versions of a code of ethics: The case study of the Israel Broadcasting Authority.* Paper presented at the annual conference of the Association for Education in Journalism and Mass Communication, New Orleans, LA.

Limor, Y., & Nossek, H. (2000). The "monkey trial" in the land of the Bible: Modern techniques of religious censorship—the case study of Israel. In Y. Kamalipour & J. Thierstein (Eds.), *Religion law and freedom: A global perspective* (pp. 63–80). Westport, CT: Greenwood.

Merrill, J. C. (1974). *The imperative of freedom.* New York: Hastings House.

Merrill, J. C. (1991a). Journalists are essentially unethical. In E. Dennis & J. C. Merrill (Eds.), *Media debates* (pp. 151–154). New York: Longman.

Merrill, J. C. (1991b). Press councils and ethical codes are dangerous control mechanisms. In E. Dennis & J. C. Merrill (Eds.), *Media debates* (pp. 161–164). New York: Longman.

Moore, W. (1970). *The professions: Roles and rules.* New York: Russell Sage Foundation.

Pasqua, T. (1990). *Mass media in the information age.* Englewood Cliffs, NJ: Prentice Hall.

Reuss, C. (1996). Media ethics codes are important and too often they are facades that imply ethical behavior. In D. Gordon, J. Kittross, & C. Reuss (Eds.), *Controversies in media ethics* (pp. 63–79). White Plains, NY: Longman.

Richeri, G. (1986). *Television from service to business: European tendencies and the Italian case.* In P. Drummond & R. Paterson (Eds.), *Television in transition* (pp. 21–35). London: BFI.

Rogel, N. (1972). *Tadrich Le-Ovdei Hahadashot Ve-Hareportaja* [Guidelines for broadcasting news and current affairs]. Jerusalem: Israel Broadcasting Authority. (Mimeographed).

Rogel, N. (1979). *Tadrich Hadashot Ve-Aktualia* [Guidelines for broadcasting news and current affairs]. Jerusalem: Israel Broadcasting Authority. (Mimeographed).

Rogel, N. (1985). *Tadrich Hadashot Ve-Aktualia* [Guidelines for broadcasting news and current affairs]. Jerusalem: Israel Broadcasting Authority. (Mimeographed).

Rogel, N. (1998). *Tadrich Nakdi: Tadrich Hadashot Ve-Aktualia* [Guidelines for broadcasting news and current affairs]. Jerusalem: Israel Broadcasting Authority.

Rogel, N., & Schejter, A. (1995). *Mismach Nakdi: Tadrich Hadashot Ve-Aktualia* [Guidelines for broadcasting news and current affairs]. Jerusalem: Israel Broadcasting Authority.

Rolland, A., & Ostbye, H. (1986). Breaking the broadcasting monopoly. In D. McQuail & K. Siune (Eds.), *New media politics* (pp. 115–129). London: Sage.

Shalit, D. (1995, November 24). Anachnu Lo Smolanim [We are not leftists]. *Haíaretz,* pp. 32–34.

Siebert, F., Peterson, T., & Schramm, W. (1963). *Four theories of the press.* Urbana: University of Illinois Press. (Originally published in 1956)

Sonninen, P., & Laitila, T. (1995). Press councils in Europe. In K. Nordenstreng (Ed.), *Reports on media ethics in Europe* (pp. 3–22). Tampere, Finland: Department of Journalism and Mass Communication, University of Tampere.

Tracey, M. (1998). *The decline and fall of public service broadcasting.* Oxford, England: Oxford University Press.

Trikha, N. K. (1986). *The press council: A self-regulatory mechanism for the press.* Bombay, India: Somaiya Publications.

Journal of Mass Media Ethics, 17(2), 155–173
Copyright © 2002, Lawrence Erlbaum Associates, Inc.

Leaks: How Do Codes of Ethics Address Them?

Taegyu Son
University of North Carolina at Chapel Hill

❏ *In this article I analyze how journalistic codes of ethics in the United States wrestle with the matter of leaks. After assessing how leaks—particularly from government sources—can compromise journalistic independence, I discuss strengths and weakness of ethics codes. Four research questions are explored via a systematic analysis of 47 codes. Although leaks are never explicitly addressed in these codes, the treatment of confidential sources and the need to maintain journalistic independence are addressed.*

On November 4, 2000, then President Bill Clinton vetoed the Intelligence Authorization Act for 2001 because of what he termed "one badly flawed provision."[1] The provision, designed to prevent and punish government leaks, had been requested by the Central Intelligence Agency (CIA). In vetoing the act, however, Clinton recognized the basic conflict inherent in government leaks, a conflict between legitimate government interests in secrecy and the public's right to know:

> I agree that unauthorized disclosures can be extraordinarily harmful to United States national security interests and that far too many such disclosures occur. … Unauthorized disclosures damage our intelligence relationships abroad, compromise intelligence gathering, jeopardize lives, and increase the threat of terrorism.

However, Clinton stressed the need also to recognize a countervailing interest—"the rights of citizens to receive the information necessary for democracy to work." The antileak law, said Clinton, "does not achieve the proper balance."[2]

Although the president focused on balancing national security concerns and the public's right to know, journalists opposed to the antileak provision raised practical concerns. "Any effort to impose criminal sanctions for disclosing classified information must confront the reality that the 'leak' is an important instrument of communication that is employed on a routine basis by officials at every level of government," chief executives of major news organization[3] said in a letter to Clinton urging him to veto the provision.[4]

Yet the bill resurfaced nearly a year after it died from Clinton's veto. On September 6, 2001, the bill was once again unanimously approved by the Senate Select Committee on Intelligence. However, the bill contained a provision requiring the U.S. Attorney General to submit the results of the administration's review of "the problem of leaks of classified information" to Congress no later than May 1, 2002.[5]

The battle over the antileak provision demonstrates the seriousness of the problem. Without sources, there would be no news stories. Encountering the high wall of secrecy in the government, U.S. journalists often rely on leaks to obtain information. In some respects, receiving leaked information has become an inevitable survival technique for journalists to attain and retain standing in their profession. An obsession with exclusivity compels journalists to rely excessively on leaks. Obtaining a scoop enables a journalist to prove his or her ability. A reporter profits by appearing to be more enterprising and better informed than his or her colleagues or competitors.

But leaking of specific information is also an important means for the government to control the media (Malek, 1997, pp. 9–10). Richard Halloran (1983), a former *New York Times* Pentagon reporter, asserted that leaking is "a political instrument wielded almost daily by senior officials within the Administration to influence a decision, to promote policy, to persuade Congress and to signal foreign governments. Leaks are oil in the machinery of government" (p. A16). Some leaks are used to influence an internal struggle within the government. Reporters are aware that officials are using them, but, in exchange for the information journalists need to produce the exclusives and scoops, they allow government sources to use them.

Independence, however, is one of the principles of the journalistic profession. In fact, it is one of the four guiding principles of the code of ethics of the nation's largest organization of journalists, the Society of Professional Journalists, and it appears in most news media codes. Conrad Fink (1995) argued, "Principled journalists make every effort to remain free of any association, ideology, group or person that might restrict freedom of the press or their personal freedom to cover the news as it must be covered" (p. 13). During the late 18th and early 19th centuries, U.S. journalism was considered "a common component of the government" (Oswald, 1994, p. 389, n. 23). Even though freedom of the press was considered an important professional concern, independent and autonomous reporting were not. But in the 20th century independence from the government became an important value in U.S. journalism circles. A collaborative press–government relationship is "no longer deemed desirable or acceptable by most citizens." (Oswald, 1994, p. 389, n. 23). Fink (1995) emphasized the following:

> Being independent is, really, fundamental to all principles so firmly held by journalists. Reporters whose conduct or associations compromise their inde-

pendence and integrity cannot pretend to serve the public or act as stewards of the First Amendment or, obviously, be fair and balanced. (p. 18)

In the United States, the press's watchdog role over the government is "rooted in a provision of the First Amendment through which the Framers sought to ensure press independence" (Onorato, 1986, p. 361). The First Amendment, which is the most significant legal protection for freedom of the press, serves "to insulate the press from the government to enable the press to perform its Fourth Estate role" (Bezanson, 1977, pp. 752–754). In that context, leaks symbolize one of the most serious moral dilemmas of U.S. journalists. While voicing allegiance to journalistic autonomy and ethical standards consistent with the First Amendment guarantee, U.S. journalists nonetheless allow government officials to manage the news and manipulate news stories through leaks. To maintain their competitiveness, journalists willingly become the government's managerial tool, often ignoring fundamental precepts of journalism ethics—independence and the fourth branch function. As John Merrill (1990) noted, "Reporters and editors are usually willing to cooperate in their own manipulation by government. The press seldom tries to provide its audience with the real story behind the leaks" (pp. 182–183).

> *While voicing allegiance to journalistic autonomy and ethical standards consistent with the First Amendment guarantee, U.S. journalists nonetheless allow government officials to manage the news and manipulate news stories through leaks.*

This article analyzes the way journalistic codes of ethics in the United States wrestle with the matter of leaks. Do journalistic ethics codes recognize the conflict caused by leaks? Do they provide any guidance for dealing with leaks and leakers?

Although the effectiveness of codes of ethics has been the subject of considerable debate, codes of ethics in journalism are one avenue to understanding and evaluating journalism standards and values. David Boeyink (1994) has argued, "While a variety of mechanisms of accountability have been advocated, codes of ethics have been the most widely used" (p. 893). And according to Abbott (1983), "Ethics codes are the most concrete cultural form in which professions acknowledge their societal obligation" (p. 856). Analyzing journalistic codes of ethics can help reveal what notions and perceptions journalists in the United States have about leaks, which are one of the most important moral dilemmas they face.

Literature Review

The literature that provides the foundation for this study can be placed in two categories: (a) literature discussing leaks that focuses on the definition of the term, the use of leaks by officials, and the negative impact of leaks on both government and journalism; and (b) studies of codes of ethics that examine what functions codes of ethics have for journalists and what codes of ethics should say about journalistic practices.

Leaks

Anonymity is an inevitable element of news leaks. Every leaker is an anonymous or unnamed source, but not every anonymous source is a leaker. The most important difference between leakers and other anonymous sources lies in the process of getting the information. Richard Kielbowicz (1979/1980) said

> The term "leak," coined in the early twentieth century, was originally applied to inadvertent slips in which information was picked up by reporters. The word quickly acquired a broader, more active meaning: any calculated release of information to reporters with the stipulation that the source remains unidentified. (p. 53)

Most authors use the term *leaks* to refer only to information provided by government officials.

Differentiating leakers from backgrounders, which are also anonymous sources, Leon Sigal (1973) said that in leaks, "the official deals with reporters as individuals, never in a group. ... The contact is non-routine and initiated by the officials. Some background briefings are held on a regular basis at the instigation of the reporters themselves" (p. 144). Martin Linsky (1991) explained that "a leaker is more regularly someone who takes the initiative with the journalists; an anonymous source is a person the journalist contacts, often routinely, for information and insight" (p. 170). To support his definition, Linsky quoted Albert Hunt, then Washington bureau chief for the *Wall Street Journal*, "Leaks are stories that are instigated, sometimes by the government, for a purpose" (p. 170). Melvin Mencher (1997) added, "The leak is one of the instruments of government. ... The other common characteristic of the leak is that it serves the leaker's purpose" (p. 313). The line drawn between leakers and general anonymous sources is based on whether the contact is initiated by the official or the journalist, as well as the source's motivation in providing information.

Leaks can be categorized according to the leaker's motivations.

Stephen Hess (1984) identified six categories of leaks according to the leaker's motivations:

1. The ego leak: giving information primarily to satisfy a sense of self-importance.
2. The goodwill leak: a play for a future favor.
3. The policy leak: a straightforward pitch for or against a proposal using some document or insider's information.
4. The animus leak: information is disclosed to embarrass another person.
5. The trial-balloon leak: revealing a proposal that is under consideration to assess its assets and liabilities.
6. The whistle-blower leak: going to the press may be the last resort of frustrated civil servants who feel they cannot correct a perceived wrong through regular government channels. (pp. 77–78)

According to Hess (1984), some leaks "promote the public good," whereas others "injure the public good. … Leaks qua leaks, then, are not an unalloyed good, although they are a means of protest that is justified for some types of dissenters who do need protection" (pp. 92–93). Overall, however, Hess's evaluation of leaks was negative. He warned that "in management terms, leaks or the threat of leaks may lead to hurried or conspiratorial decision making" (p. 93).

The animus leak is a tool of immoral political players. Animus leakers exploit reporters as conveyors of disinformation. A reporter who is eager only to receive credit for scoops does not much concern himself or herself about the character of the leaked information—rumor or disinformation. According to Tom Goldstein (1985), the animus leak often occurs between prosecutors and reporters:

> When prosecutors leak to journalists, journalists invariably get manipulated, and the target of the leak usually gets unfair treatment by being stigmatized in the press. Most of the time, reporters do not understand or try to discover the motive of a prosecutor, and it is rare that officials confer benefits on re-

porters without some selfish motive. Occasionally a prosecutor who is unable to secure an indictment under the rules of evidence seeks to harm his target by means of unfavorable publicity. He will leak derogatory information about such a target to reporters grateful to get exclusives and who proceed to injure someone who, at least in the eyes of the law, is not culpable. (p. 50)

Goldstein's explanation detailed the symbiotic relation between leakers who have animus purpose and reporters who are obsessed with exclusivity.

Because of these functions of leaks, they have been characterized by many scholars as harmful and unacceptable behavior of government officials and journalists. Sigal (1973) presented leaks as a weapon wielded to enhance the bargaining position of an official or a policy position. Tant (1995) defined a *leak* as "the unauthorized disclosure of secret government information" (p. 197) and labeled leaks as "acts of irresponsibility or betrayal" (p. 197). Reporting on the leaking of information from President Clinton's deposition in the sexual harassment case Paula Jones filed, Warren Richey (1998) asserted the following:

From a journalistic perspective, such news reports are dangerous because a leak may not be accurate and most likely reflects the undisclosed bias of the leaker. From a legal perspective, such a flood of leaks in the face of a protective order by a federal judge suggests a lack of respect for the law and the legal process. (p. 1)

Daniel Schorr (1998) pointed out that leaks can have legal as well as moral ramifications for journalists: "It is a crime to leak grand jury information. Although it is not a crime for a reporter to receive such information, theoretically he or she could be called as a witness to a crime" (p. 3).

For Eleanor Randolph (1989), however, a key danger of leaks is that they undermine journalistic independence.

A leak from a high-level official is more often a strategic move to help formulate or further a policy, and many journalists fear that they are being used as part of the process rather than as disinterested reporters relaying facts to the public. (p. 44)

In sum, unlike general anonymous sources, leakers can be defined as sources, primarily government officials, who want to exploit reporters for their own purposes, giving exclusive information that is sometimes rumor or disinformation.

Codes of Ethics

Despite the growing numbers of news media codes of ethics, their effectiveness has been continually debated. Noting that "social scientists have repeatedly found that there is little correlation between ethical beliefs and ethical behavior," Flink (1997) argued, "For journalists a written ethical code is comforting, high-minded, and impractical. It may be employed as a shield—'We do things right, read our code.' Or at best it is a reminder—often eloquently composed—of ineffable inside" (p. 259).

David Pritchard and Madelyn Morgan (1989) sought to measure the effectiveness of written codes of ethics. They concluded,

> The adoption of ethics codes should not necessarily be expected to make journalists more ethical. … The results of this study provide no support for the assumption that ethics codes directly influence the decisions journalists make. … It may be that the most important effects of ethics codes are symbolic, rather than behavioral. (pp. 934, 941)

However, several scholars have discussed the useful functions of media codes of ethics from a normative perspective. David Gordon (1999), a proponent of ethics codes, argued the following:

> Written codes help acquaint media neophytes with some of the key ethical issues and principles they will face as practitioners. … More generally, codes can sharpen the focus on ethical issues that people in all branches of the media must face regularly. (p. 63)

Gordon defended codes of ethics from criticism over lack of enforcement, "Ethics, by its nature, deals with what should happen rather than what can be legalistically enforced" (p. 64). Tom Goldstein (1985) expressed doubt about the effectiveness of codes of ethics because "the gap between the admirable sentiments expressed in the codes and the way journalists actually behave is wide indeed," but he also acknowledged their usefulness for journalism neophytes: "Codes can be useful, especially for young journalists, in setting out what situations represent conflicts of interest and what do not, in explaining what plagiarism is," and in setting forth an organization's policy on such subjects as posing, the use of anonymous sources, or the secret taping of conversations (p. 167).

While mentioning the educational function of codes, Jay Black (1996) pointed out their usefulness not only for media newcomers, but also for media veterans. He wrote,

> A good code promotes ethical thought and behavior within a profession. This is especially important for newcomers, who may not know the complexity of the craft's moral land mines. But it is also of value for veterans faced with pressures from the peers and higher-ups to violate a profession's values and norms. (p. 24)

Deni Elliot-Boyle (1985/1986) added the following:

U.S. journalists, like members of every other formal or informal group, operate within a set of understood conventions that govern behavior. … While
codes can provide working journalists with statements of minimums and
perceived ideals, the codes can also help journalists abstract and articulate
these understood conventions of the business. (p. 25)

Andrew Belsey and Ruth Chadwick (1999) noted that, "an ethical code
of practice will have both positive and negative aspects, detailing what is
required and what is prohibited. Both aspects clearly have a contribution
to make to media quality." They provided examples of both types of code
provisions:

A code of practice for the media, for example, could require journalists to be
honest and accurate in all matters, to be impartial and objective in reporting
news, to publish corrections, to offer a right of reply, to protect the identity of
confidential sources. It could also, presumably, prohibit deception, harassment, invasions of privacy, doorstepping the victims of traumatic events, ex-
ploiting children, buying the stories of criminals. (p. 61)

In his case study of the *Courier-Journal* in Louisville, Kentucky, Boeyink
(1998) concluded that the paper's "ethical standards were not public relations tools but working principles that shaped frequent ethical discussion
and helped determine behavior" (p. 180).

---

*Although they are criticized
or being emblematic and
impractical, codes of ethics
have been the most widely
used mechanism for
journalistic accountability.*

Nevertheless, some scholars have contended that codes of ethics for
journalists merely advocate ideal standards of behavior and lack practical
value. Niegel Harris (1992) argued, "Many existing codes present lists of
the types of action which are to be avoided, but say relatively little about
what would constitute good practice and how it might be achieved" (p.
75). Philip Seib and Kathy Fitzpatrick (1997) suggested the following:

Codes should explain the ethical philosophy behind ethical behavior such
that journalists are stimulated to think about not only what is right or wrong,

but also why it is right or wrong. Rather than simply providing a list of *dos* and *don'ts*, codes should articulate the importance of adhering to ethical norms. (pp. 14–15)

In summary, although they are criticized for being emblematic and impractical, codes of ethics have been the most widely used mechanism for journalistic accountability. Codes of ethics are expected to upgrade the behavior of journalists.

Research Questions and Method

To study whether journalistic ethics codes recognize the conflict caused by leaks and whether they provide any guidance for dealing with leaks and leakers, this article addresses the following questions:

1. Do journalistic codes of ethics directly or explicitly address the handling of leaks as an ethical issue? If so, how? What guidelines within the codes address dealing with leaked information and its sources?
2. Do codes of ethics implicitly address the handling of leaks? If so, how? What guidance do these provisions provide journalists in deciding whether and how to use leaked information?
3. How do codes of ethics that neither explicitly nor implicitly address the handling of leaks guide journalists in dealing with anonymous sources or confidential sources?
4. Do codes of ethics have sections discussing journalistic independence, which has been said to be hindered by leaks? If so, how do the codes guide journalists to establish relationships with their sources to maintain journalistic independence?

Overall, 47 codes of ethics were assembled for this study. Among them are codes of ethics from the American Society of Newspaper Editors (ASNE), Society of Professional Journalists, the Associated Press, Gannett, the *New York Times,* the *Los Angeles Times,* and the *Washington Post.* The study uses every code submitted to ASNE,[6] a total of 39, and two additional codes collected by the Center for the Study of Ethics in the Professions.[7] The other six were gathered by the author, who independently contacted a dozen news organizations and asked for their codes of ethics (see Table 1).

The author carefully analyzed the content of all 47 codes first to determine whether they directly or explicitly mentioned the term *leak* or *leaker.* Next each code was examined for implicit or indirect references. This entailed searching for phrases that could relate to leaks or leakers, such as references to the unauthorized disclosure of secret government information,

Table 1. Codes of Ethics Analyzed

Arizona Republic (Phoenix)
Asbury Park Press (Neptune, New Jersey), Our code of ethics
American Society of Newspaper Editors, Statement of Principles
Associated Press Managing Editors, Code of Ethics
Atlanta Journal-Constitution (Atlanta, Georgia), Ethics Code
Chicago Tribune Company, Editorial Ethics Policy
Christian Science Monitor (Boston, Massachusetts), Ethical Standards
Daily Press (Newport News, Virginia), Statement of Journalistic Ethics
Dallas Morning News, News Department Guidelines
Des Moines Register and *Tribune,* Code of Ethics
Deseret News (Salt Lake City, Utah), Code of Ethics
E. W. Scripps Company, Statement of Policy on Ethics and Professional Conduct
Gannett Newspaper Division
Gazette (Cedar Rapids, Iowa), Code of Ethics
Hartford Courant (Hartford, Connecticut), News Ethics Code, Business News Ethics Policy,
    Sports Ethics Code
Herald Times (Bloomington, Indiana), Newsroom Code
Honolulu Advertiser (Honolulu, Hawaii), Principles of Ethical Conduct
Houston Chronicle, Human Resources Guide
Journal Gazette (Fort Wayne, Indiana), Ethics Policy
Journal News (White Plains, New York), Standards of Professional Conduct for news
    employees
Kansas City (Mo.) Star, Conflicts of interest
Lincoln (Neb.) Journal Star, Ethics Code
Los Angeles Times, Code of Ethics
Milwaukee Journal, Rules and Guidelines
News-Gazette (Champaign, Illinois), Guidelines for Professional Standards
News Journal (Newcastle, Delaware), Code of Professionalism and Ethics
News & Observer (Raleigh, North Carolina), Ethics Policy
News-Times (Danbury, Connecticut), Ethics Code
New York Times, Guidelines on Our Integrity
Orlando (Fla.) Sentinel, Editorial Code of Ethics
Philadelphia Inquirer, Conflicts of interest
Pittsburgh Post-Gazette, Statement of Policy
Record (Hackensack, New Jersey), An Ethics Code
Richmond Times-Dispatch, Guidelines For Professional Conduct
Roanoke (Va.) Times, News and Editorial Mission and Vision
Radio-Television News Directors Association (RTNDA), Codes of Ethics and Standards
Society of American Business Editors and Writers (SABEW), Code of Ethics
San Francisco Chronicle, Ethical News Gathering
San Jose Mercury News, Ethics: A Statement of Principles
Seattle Times, Newsroom Policies and Guidelines
Society of Professional Journalists (SPJ), Code of Ethics
Statements Journal (Salem, Oregon), Newsroom Ethics Policy
Tampa Tribune (Tampa, Florida), Newsroom Ethics Policy
Tribune-Democrat (Johnstown, Pennsylvania), Codes of Ethics
Washington Post, Standards and Ethics
Wisconsin State Journal (Madison), Codes of Ethics
York (Pa.) Daily Record, Guide to your workplace

any calculated release of information, or government officials who want to exploit or manipulate reporters, sources who attempt to influence news coverage through the release of information. Third, each code was reviewed to determine whether it included any mention of confidential, anonymous sources or unnamed sources, and if so, how it dealt with that topic. Finally, each code was examined to identify references to journalistic source–journalist relationships.

Findings

Research Question 1

Do journalistic codes of ethics directly or explicitly address the handling of leaks as an ethical issue? If so, how? What guidelines within the codes address dealing with leaked information and its sources?

None of the 47 codes of ethics analyzed for this study directly mentions leaks. Of the 47 codes of ethics analyzed, 16, including those of the *Los Angeles Times,* Associated Press, Chicago Tribune Company, the *Atlanta Journal-Constitution,* and the *Philadelphia Inquirer,* do not even mention sources.[8] For instance, the code of the *Atlanta Journal-Constitution* begins by saying that "newspapers function as a watchdog on government and other institutions," but it never deals with the matter of sources, to say nothing of the matter of leaks.

Although 31 of the 47 codes discuss *sources, anonymous sources,* or *unnamed sources,* no code uses the term *leaks* or *leaker.* Most codes that have sections on sources stress that the use of an anonymous source can lessen the credibility of the story and the institution, but they do not mention leaks.

Research Question 2

Do codes of ethics implicitly address the handling of leaks? If so, how? What guidance do these provisions provide journalists in deciding whether and how to use leaked information?

Only 6 of the 31 codes that discuss sources indirectly or implicitly deal with leakers. These codes do not use the term *leaks,* but they warn news employees not to be used by anonymous sources with animus purposes or advise reporters and editors to pay attention to anonymous sources' motivations. For instance, the Gannett code provides these guidelines concerning anonymous sources with questionable motives:

> Do not allow unnamed sources to take cheap shots in stories. It is unfair and unprofessional. Expect reporters and editors to seek to understand the moti-

vations of a source and take those into account in evaluating the fairness and truthfulness of the information provided.

The Gannett code urges reporters and editors to check the purposes of unnamed sources. Although the code does not use the term *leaks*, the guidelines imply that reporters and editors should not be exploited by leakers.

The ethics code of the *Journal News* in White Plains, New York, likewise states, "The motive of the anonymous source should be fully examined to prevent our being used unwittingly to grind someone's ax." The code of the *Daily Press* in Newport News, Virginia, declares, "Unnamed sources are best avoided, particularly where the information they provide is somehow accusatory." The *New York Times* code also tersely mentions, "The general rule is to tell readers as much as we can about the placement and known motivation of the source." The code of the *Tampa Tribune* simply advises: "Be skeptical of a source's motives and be fair: Don't permit anonymous character attacks."

The Society of Professional Journalists code contains several statements that could have relevance for the handling of leaks. One warns, "Be wary of sources offering information for favors." The favors, of course, that leakers want are the very disclosure of their information in the manner and at the time they choose. That section also tells journalists to resist pressure from advertisers and special interests "to influence news coverage." Government leakers would seem to qualify as "special interests" who attempt "to influence news coverage."

Research Question 3

How do codes of ethics that neither explicitly nor implicitly address the handling of leaks guide journalists in dealing with anonymous sources or confidential sources?

Most of the other 25 codes that mention anonymous sources urge editors and reporters to disclose the identity of sources whenever they can, although they do not explicitly or implicitly wrestle with the matter of leaks. In addition, most of the 25 codes stress protecting confidential sources. Some media institutions note the importance of anonymous sources for their news gathering, but they do not call their employees' attention to the negative aspects of anonymous sources.

The *Washington Post* code says about sources,

> *The Post* is pledged to disclose the source of all information when at all possible. When we agree to protect a source's identity, that identity will not be made known to anyone outside *The Post*. ... Before any information is ac-

cepted without full attribution, reporters must make every reasonable effort
to get it on the record.

But *The Post* does not mention examining the motivations and purposes
of informants who seek anonymity.

The Radio–Television News Directors Association (RTNDA) 2000 code
instructs professional electronic journalists as follows:

> Identify sources whenever possible. Confidential sources should be used
> only when it is clearly in the public interest to gather or convey important in-
> formation or when a person providing information might be harmed. Jour-
> nalists should keep all commitments to protect a confidential source.

The *Wisconsin State Journal* code advises that using "unattributed quotations is strongly discouraged and must be cleared with the editor or managing editor." It also stresses that *"State Journal's* staffers acknowledge the
journalists' ethic of protecting confidential sources of information."

The ASNE code briefly mentions sources: "Pledges of confidentiality to
news sources must be honored at all costs. … Unless there is clear and
pressing need to maintain confidences, sources of information should be
identified." The *Arizona Republic* code emphasizes protecting confidential
sources in the segment on sources: "Reporters should not make a pledge or
promise of confidentiality they are not empowered to honor and enforce,
and editors should honor promises properly made by reporters." The *Richmond Times-Dispatch* code's main concern is also the protection of anonymous sources. It states, "Pledges of anonymity to news sources should be
made sparingly with the utmost caution and ideally after consultation between reporter and editor. … A pledge of anonymity by a reporter or editor
will be honored by the *Times-Dispatch."*

The *Orlando Sentinel* code stresses that "the use of anonymous sources
should be avoided because it undermines the newspaper's credibility." It
also details how to deal with various anonymous sources, "Reporters
should be careful to note the distinction between information provided on
the record, on background and off the record." But the *Orlando Sentinel*
code does not differentiate leaks from other anonymous sources. The *San
Francisco Chronicle* states,

> The use of confidential sources should be the exception rather than the rou-
> tine. … The decision to use a confidential source can lessen the credibility of
> the story and the newspaper. … A reporter who pledges confidentiality to a
> source must not violate that pledge.

In particular, the *Chronicle* code says that "editors and reporters should
seriously consider the value of information received from a confidential

source before deciding to print it." The *Chronicle* guidelines only note "the value of information," not the character of information, that is, whether it is leaked information.

Research Question 4

Do codes of ethics have sections discussing journalistic independence, which has been said to be hindered by leaks? If so, how do the codes guide journalists to establish relationships with their sources to maintain journalistic independence?

Although ethics code provisions addressing sources, especially confidential sources, seem to be the most likely place for journalists to look for guidance in dealing with leaks, code sections discussing journalistic autonomy and independence might also be expected to provide some guidelines given the widespread recognition in the literature that leaks are a way for officials to manipulate and use the media. Forty-five of the 47 codes analyzed for this study contain provisions directly or indirectly referring to journalistic independence. However, none of the 45 codes that mention independence directly or indirectly ever explicitly recognizes that leaks might be a threat to that value and journalists should not allow themselves to be a managerial tool of officials through leaks. Those codes generally emphasize the normative value of journalistic independence whereas some stress journalists are not to accept any gifts or favors from sources.

The ASNE code says that its members "should neither accept anything nor pursue any activity that might compromise or seem to compromise their integrity." The Associated Press Managing Editors code also states, in the section titled "Independence," that "the newspaper and its staff should be free of obligation to news sources and newsmakers. Even the appearance of obligation or conflict of interest should be avoided. Newspapers should accept nothing of value from news sources." The *Kansas City Star* code instructs its editorial employees that they "must aggressively seek and fully report the truth while remaining independent and free from any legitimate suggestion that their independence has been compromised." The *Roanoke Times* code briefly says that "the independence of our editors, reporters and photographers is not for sale."

The *Philadelphia Inquirer* code stresses that "a staff member may not receive payment from anyone or any organization that he or she might he expected to cover or make news judgments about." The code of the *Deseret News* in Salt Lake City, Utah, says that "no employee should accept a gift ... or any other benefit in exchange for a promise—implied or otherwise—to place or influence a story in the newspaper."

Relating to journalistic independence, the code of the *Journal News* in White Plains, New York, specifically mentions government control: "To warrant the public's trust, a newspaper must be free of governmental control and official coercion." The code of the *Hartford Courant* in Connecticut acknowledges that reporters rely heavily on officials for news and tips. It advises reporters not to take "gifts of any kind and not to accept favors, such as an offer by a municipal official to void a parking ticket" while developing "good working relationships with many sources." Neither code advises journalists to be wary of officials using the calculated disclosure of information to control them.

The 47 U.S. codes of journalism ethics analyzed for this study never use the term leaks and never explicitly wrestle with the matter of leaks.

Discussions and Conclusion

The 47 U.S. codes of journalism ethics analyzed for this study never use the term *leaks* and never explicitly wrestle with the matter of leaks. Only 6 of the 47 codes implicitly address handling leaks, but they do not provide journalists adequate guidance in deciding whether and how to use leaked information. Those codes just warn their reporters and editors to pay attention to their sources' purposes or motivations, even though they discuss in some detail gifts, favors, or special treatment from sources.

In particular, journalists' use of leaks relates to two main issues addressed in at least some codes of ethics: the proper use of confidential sources and the need to maintain journalistic independence. The problem, however, is that none of the codes draws the necessary connection between those two provisions to provide guidance to reporters and editors dealing with leakers and their often questionable motives. The code sections on confidential sources discourage the use of unnamed sources while emphasizing the need to protect the anonymity of a source once a promise of confidentiality has been made. The primary concerns of the sources' provisions seem to be, first, to maintain credibility with the audience by identifying sources whenever possible and, second, to keep promises made to sources.

The independence provisions, on the other hand, warn journalists to avoid being manipulated and used, urge them to avoid outside pressures, and caution against conduct that compromises journalistic integrity. However, the focus of those sections tends to be accepting gifts, favors, and special treatment, conflicts of interest, and potential pressures created by advertisers. The link between autonomy and sources, especially leakers, is not made. Even though 45 of the 47 codes analyzed for this study address journalistic autonomy, no code explicitly emphasizes independence from leakers.

Leaks are an important element in the relationship between journalists and government officials. Using leaks also reflects on the character of journalism. Therefore, political science and journalism scholars have studied the matter of leaks. And despite hot debates over their effectiveness, codes of ethics are one avenue to identifying journalists' ethical principles and concerns. Codes of ethics "reflect the various ways American newspapers address matters of ethics" (Steele, 2000).

Leaks, however, are not addressed in journalistic codes of ethics as much as they should be. Why? It may be, on the one hand, the result of journalists' attitude toward leaks. In a 1980 survey of journalists, 87% said the use of leaks was a good practice.[9] The letter that chief executives of four of the largest news organizations wrote to President Clinton opposing the antileak law provides an important clue to understanding U.S. journalists' perception of leaks. The executives of prominent media institutions defined *leaks* not as the managerial tool of government officials but as an important instrument of communication by officials. Their definition is strikingly different from the definition of many scholars. Regardless of scholarly criticism of leaks, most journalists favor leaks. For them, leaking is not an "act of irresponsibility or betrayal" or a crime, causing them an ethical dilemma. Journalists seem to consider leakers to be not traitors in government but persons who want to reveal corruption or duplicity. Those perceptions might be one reason journalists ignore the subject of leaks in their codes of ethics.

On the other hand, the code writers might have believed the central issue of leaking is part of those sections that deal with broader issues, such as independence and anonymous sources, of which leaks are just one important example. Further research could reveal more exact reasons.

As members of the press dig deeper to get to the truth of events in government, anonymous sources increase. Journalists without confidential sources are no more than soldiers without weapons. But the more journalists grant anonymity to sources without verifying their bias, calculation, and purpose, the more often they sink to being government's managerial tool, putting journalists on slippery moral ground. Journalistic independence cannot be truly achieved if journalists receive information from government leakers who attempt "to influence news coverage" for favors— the very disclosure of their information in the manner and at the time they choose.

A code of ethics promotes ethical thought and behavior within a profession. The *Christian Science Monitor* code articulates the need for codes of ethics: "Without explicit standards, good men and women can disagree on what is the most ethical course of action under a given set of circumstances." Codifying the definition of *leaks* and creating guidelines for avoiding being manipulated by leakers will lessen the danger of their moral ambiguity. At a minimum, codes of ethics should acknowledge that leaks are often a tool of government officials with self-interests, and they should advise journalists to discard any leaked information from officials with animus purposes.

Notes

1. President Clinton's statement. Quoted in Radio–Television News Directors Association (2000) news release.
2. President Clinton's statement. Quoted in Radio–Television News Directors Association (2000) news release.
3. *CNN,* the *Washington Post,* the Newspaper Association of America, and the *New York Times.*
4. Quoted in *New York Times,* November 1, 2000, p. A29.
5. News release of the Senate Select Committee on Intelligence, September 6, 2001. It said:

> The bill, as marked-up by the Committee, also contains a provision requiring further study about the problem of leaks of classified information. Because the Attorney General requested that the Committee not take any legislative action on the issue of the unauthorized disclosure of classified information until the Administration can conduct a thorough interagency review of this matter, the bill contains a provision codifying the Attorney General's proposal, and requiring the Attorney General to submit the unclassified results of this review to Congress no later than May 1, 2002. The report of the Attorney General's review shall include, among other things, an assessment of the efficacy and adequacy of current laws and regulations against the unauthorized disclosure of classified information, including whether or not modifications of such laws or regulations, or additional laws or regulations, are advisable in order to further protect against the unauthorized disclosure of such information.

6. Retrieved February 6, 2001 at MACROBUTTON HtmlResAnchor http://www.asne.org/ideas/codes/codes.htm. ASNE last updated this page on December 13, 2000.
7. Retrieved September 7, 2000 at MACROBUTTON HtmlResAnchor http://csep.iit.edu/codes/coe/.
8. The others are *Des Moines Register and Tribune;* E. W. Scripps Company; *Gazette* in Cedar Rapids, Iowa; *Herald-Times* in Bloomington, Indiana; *Houston Chronicle; Journal Gazette* in Fort Wayne, Indiana; *News-Times* in Danbury, Connecti-

cut; *Pittsburgh Post-Gazette; Seattle Times;* Society of American Business Editors and Writers; and *Tribune-Democrat* in Johnstown, Pennsylvania.

9. See Culbertson (1980). In his article, while explaining the results of the survey of journalists, Culbertson wrote, "About 81% of them felt unnamed sources were less believable, on the whole, than named. Yet 87% said the use of leaks is, on balance, a good practice" (p. 402).

References

Abbott, A. (1983). Professional ethics. *American Journal of Sociology, 88,* 855–885.

Belsey, A., & Chadwick, R. (1999). Ethics as a vehicle for media quality. In R. M. Baird, W. E. Loges, & S. E. Rosenbaum (Eds.), *The media & morality* (pp. 55–67). New York: Prometheus.

Bezanson, R. (1977). The new free press guarantee. *Virginia Law Review, 63,* 731–788.

Black, J. (1996). Now that we have the ethics code, how do we use it? *Quill, 84,* 24–25.

Boeyink, D. E. (1994). How effective are codes of ethics? A look at three newsrooms. *Journalism Quarterly, 71,* 893–904.

Boeyink, D. E. (1998). Codes and culture at the *Courier-Journal:* Complexity in ethical decision making. *Journal of Mass Media Ethics, 13,* 165–182.

Culbertson, H. (1980). Leaks—A dilemma for editors as well as officials. *Journalism Quarterly, 57,* 402–408.

Elliot-Boyle, D. (1985/1986). A conceptual analysis of ethics codes. *Journal of Mass Media Ethics, 1,* 22–26.

Fink, C. C. (1995). *Media ethics.* Boston: Allyn & Bacon.

Flink, S. E. (1997). *Sentinel under siege: The triumphs and trouble of America's free press.* Boulder, CO: Westview Press.

Goldstein, T. (1985). *The news at any cost: How journalists compromise their ethics to shape the news.* New York: Simon & Schuster.

Gordon, D., & Kittross, J. M. (1999). *Controversies in media ethics* (2nd ed.). New York: Longman.

Halloran, R. (1983, January 14). A primer on the fine art of leaking information. *New York Times,* p. A16.

Harris, N. G. E. (1992). Codes of conduct for journalists. In A. Belsey & R. Chadwick (Eds.), *Ethical issues in journalism and media* (pp. 62–76). New York: Routledge.

Hess, S. (1984). *The government/press connection: Press officers and their offices.* Washington, DC: Brookings.

Kielbowicz, R. B. (1979/1980). Leaks to the press as communication within and between organizations. *Newspaper Research Journal, 1*(2), 53–58.

Linsky, M. (1991). *How the press affects federal policymaking.* New York: Norton.

Malek, A. (Ed.). (1997). *News media and foreign relations: A multifaceted perspective.* Norwood, NJ: Ablex.

Mencher, M. (1997). *News reporting and writing* (7th ed.) Madison, WI: Brown & Benchmark.

Merrill, J. (1990). *The imperative of freedom: A philosophy of journalistic autonomy.* New York: Freedom House.

Onorato, D. J. (1986). A press privilege for the worst of times. *Georgia Law Journal, 75,* 361–394.

Oswald, K. A. (1994). Mass media and the transformation of American politics. *Marquette Law Review, 77,* 385–414.

Pritchard, D., & Morgan, M. P. (1989). Impact of ethics codes on judgments by journalists: A natural experiment. *Journalism Quarterly, 66,* 934–941.

Radio-Television News Directors Association. (2000). News release. Retrieved November 27, 2000 from http://www.rtndf.org/news/2000/ractvall.shtml

Randolph, E. (1989, August 12). Journalists face troubling questions about leaks from criminal probes. *Washington Post,* p. A4. Quoted in Smith, R. F. (1999). *Groping for ethics in journalism* (4th ed.). Ames: Iowa State University Press.

Richey, W. (1998, February 5). Washington plays the leak game. *Christian Science Monitor,* p. 1.

Schorr, D. (1998). Leaks from the top. *New Leader, 81,* 3.

Seib, P., & Fitzpatrick, K. (1997). *Journalism ethics.* Fort Worth, TX: Harcourt Brace.

Senate Select Committee on Intelligence. (2001, September 6). Press release. Retrieved October 23, 2001 from http://intelligence.senate.gov/010906.htm

Sigal, L. V. (1973). *Reporters and officials: The organization and politics of newsmaking.* Lexington, MA: Heath.

Steele, B. (2000, September). Codes of ethics and beyond. Retrieved September 20, 2001 from http://poyter.org/research/me/coethics.htm

Tant, A. P. (1995). Leaks and the nature of British government. *The Political Quarterly, 66,* 197–209.

Journal of Mass Media Ethics, 17(2), 174–182
Copyright © 2002, Lawrence Erlbaum Associates, Inc.

Cases and Commentaries

The *Journal of Mass Media Ethics* publishes case studies in which scholars and media professionals outline how they would address a particular ethical problem. Some cases are hypothetical, but most are from actual experience in newsrooms, corporations, and agencies. We invite readers to call our attention to current cases and issues. (We have a special need for good cases in advertising and public relations.) We also invite suggestions of names of people, both professionals and academicians, who might write commentaries.

Kathy R. Fitzpatrick, DePaul University, wrote the following case.

Editor: Louis W. Hodges
Knight Professor of Ethics in Journalism
Washington and Lee University
Lexington, VA 24450

A Grassroots Initiative for the Airport

You are in charge of the public relations function for a small commercial airport located on the edge of a town with a population of about 250,000. The airport board is eager to have the town council pass a resolution that would allow it to extend the length of one of its runways so larger jets can take off and land there. The town's Chamber of Commerce supports the resolution because expanded air travel services will contribute to the economic development of the area. Area residents, on the other hand, are not happy about the increased noise pollution that would accompany the airport expansion. In an effort to gain city council approval, your boss at the airport has asked you to work with chamber officials to establish a citizens group to lobby the city council on behalf of the airport. The group, to be called Citizens for Economic Progress, will be fully funded by the airport and the chamber. However, your boss wants you to keep quiet about the source of funding so members of the city council will believe this grassroots initiative grew out of citizen concern for the development of their town. He insists that neither the airport's nor the chamber's name should appear on any printed materials. What should you do?

Commentary 1
Blind Loyalty to Client Looms Large
While Disclosure Remains the Ideal

Although we would like to say that this is an atypical case for public relations practitioners, it is not. The laws governing political action committees (PACs), for example, were passed to avoid just this type of intentional obfuscation during political campaigns. Unfortunately, too many clients still believe that this is a legitimate approach to swaying public opinion, and too many practitioners still bend too easily to client wishes.

The latest Public Relations Society of America (PRSA) Member Code of Ethics places the onus of ethical decision making squarely on the individual practitioner, where it rightly belongs. The 2000 code drastically alters the approach taken by its earlier incarnation. The code it replaced was both prescriptive and proscriptive and fell prey to the usual shortcomings inherent in most codes. It was vague when it needed to be specific and often too specific when it needed latitude.

The new code, unfortunately, suffers from much the same malaise. For our purposes, however, one of the more important elements in the earlier code has been incorporated into the 2000 revision: that dealing with disclosure of information.

The new code is what Frankel (1989) called educational in that it "seeks to buttress understanding of its provisions with extensive commentary and interpretation." The new code is divided not into articles, but into provisions. Provisions are further elucidated by defining the core principle, the intent or rationale, guidelines (all prescriptive), and examples of improper conduct under the provision.

For example, under the Disclosure of Information provision, the core principle is that "Open communication fosters informed decision making in a democratic society." The intent, or rationale, is that trust among society, the public relations practitioner, and the practitioner's client can be engendered only by revealing "all information needed for responsible decision making."

Among the guidelines listed for this code provision is an admonition to "Reveal the sponsors for causes and interests represented." And, under examples of improper conduct, the first listed is "front groups." The actual example used is, "A member implements 'grass roots' campaigns or letter-writing campaigns to legislators on behalf of undisclosed interest groups." A second relevant example is "A member deceives the public by employing people to pose as volunteers to speak at public hearings and participate in 'grass roots' campaigns." These elements of the provision of Disclosure of Information are clearly aimed at the sort of problem this case presents. The code is clear as to its intent; however, the question of blind loyalty to client interests still looms large.

The new code begins with a set of professional values, first among which is advocacy. "We serve the public interest by acting as responsible advocates for those we represent." Public interest in not defined. Perhaps one is to assume that the second point under advocacy clarifies the first. "We provide a voice in the marketplace of ideas, facts, and viewpoints to aid informed public debate." Both of these statements smack seriously of the economic model of democracy so popular for the past 200 or so years. This laissez-faire approach assumes that the public is best served by serving the client in the same way a large corporation might claim that the public is ultimately served by its economic viability: "What's good for General Motors is good for America."

This represents a departure from the previous code, which stressed neither advocacy nor counseling, both integral components of modern public relations. By focusing on advocacy, the code clearly leans toward increased client loyalty. Second to the last value cited is, in fact, loyalty. "We are faithful to those we represent, while honoring our obligation to serve the public interest." Again, public interest is not defined, nor is any information provided to explain how this juggling act might be accomplished.

As long as the profession of public relations assumes that advocacy is the primary professional value, and as long as the "public interest" remains a vague euphemism subservient to client interests under the guise of "loyalty," full disclosure of information will remain only an ideal, and tactics such as front groups will not soon disappear from the public relations bag of tricks.

Reference

Frankel, M. S. (1989). Professional codes: Why, how, and with what impact? *Journal of Business Ethics, 8,* 109–115.

By Thomas H. Bivins
Hulteng Professor of Ethics
School of Journalism and Communication
University of Oregon

Commentary 2
A Classic Catch-22 for a Conscientious Practitioner

Throughout our careers, we public relations practitioners are often challenged by ethical versus real-life dilemmas. As a guiding principle, we practitioners strive to adhere to the highest levels of professional and moral behavior on behalf of the clients and employers we represent.

This case represents a classic Catch-22 situation for a practitioner: adhering to the ethical standards of our profession while balancing the pressures of work–life reality. Although there is, perhaps, no definitive or "right" answer in resolving the conflict, the following serve as points of consideration in addressing the situation.

As with the development of any public relations strategic plan, research of the topic itself provides background and possible insight to the practitioner's situation. In recent years, community groups at various airports nationwide and globally have raised concerns regarding facility and runway expansion and the accompanying increase in noise pollution. What grassroots campaigns involving local governments, chambers of commerce, and airport boards were implemented? How did public relations efforts play key roles? In reviewing similar scenarios, the practitioner also has an opportunity to identify his or her personal perspective and bias to the cause at hand. Such attitudes can be deterrents when acting in the best interest of those we represent.

Although the ethical issue of the boss's request is the key question in this case, the practitioner's viewpoints on the value of economic expansion versus environmental effect can affect the decision-making process.

Turning now to the ethical consideration, two areas in PRSA's Code of Ethics provide relevancy and pinpoint guidelines that would be helpful to this case. Under the Disclosure of Information provision, the guidelines clearly state that a practitioner should "avoid deceptive interests" and should "reveal the sponsors for causes and interests represented." This provision even offers an example of improper conduct that parallels this specific situation: "deceiving the public by employing people to pose as volunteers to speak at public hearings and participate in 'grass roots' campaigns." The other provision, Conflicts of Interest, purports to "build trust with the public by avoiding or ending situations that put one's personal or professional interests in conflict with society's interests."

One area in PRSA's Code of Ethics, however, that proves confusing to the practitioner's case is Safeguarding Confidences, which states that a practitioner shall "safeguard the confidences ... and protect privileged [and] confidential information gained from ... an individual/organization."

On the one hand, the practitioner must build trust with the citizens' group, the city council, and other external publics, while respecting the employer's order of confidentiality.

Herein lies the crux of the practitioner's decision: the practical application of the above mentioned doctrines. The practitioner can apply the Disclosure of Information and Conflicts of Interest in the decision-making process, but what about the employer? If a professional accepts the entire Code of Ethics, then she must take into consideration the section on Safeguarding Confidences, which would require that she safeguard the confidence of her boss. This is not just an ideological issue. The practitioner must also wrestle with current job security issues, securing solid professional references in the future, or both. If this individual confronts the employer with regard to the nonethical nature of the order, what will the response be and how will it affect the practitioner?

What should the practitioner's ultimate course of action be? As public relations professionals, we know from experience that ethical situations comprise individual variables and criteria. We determine actions based on our own moral integrity, "gut" feelings, and, yes, professional guidelines.

I would like to think that this practitioner would begin to resolve the dilemma by revealing directly to the boss concerns about the deceptive behavior and the repercussions that will result. Perhaps the practitioner is able to reach a compromise without violating his integrity. Or, perhaps, as sometimes is the case, the employer will not be willing to accept the practitioner's point of view, which will force the professional to make a critical job choice.

Was the Code of Ethics, as it is currently written, helpful in this particular case? Certainly, as noted herein, it contains provisions that served as strong guidelines for the practitioner. However, the tricky area of Safeguarding Confidences needs additional guiding principles and examples to clarify situations such as this practitioner encountered.

Codes of ethics are often considered idealistic, but it is the effort to bridge idealism and practicality that raises the standards by which we function on a daily basis and ultimately enhances the public relations and all professions.

By Susan Morrow
Founder and President
Morrow & Associates, Inc.
Dallas, Texas

Commentary 3
The Ethics of Front Groups

Front groups are created by an organization that wishes to give the illusion of grassroots support for an issue. Some agencies commonly advertise that they can generate "grassroots support" almost instantaneously, a public relations technique often called "Astroturf." Although this might be a common practice, it is not necessarily morally sound.

The practitioner in this case should start by analyzing PRSA's Member Code of Ethics 2000. The code outlines the Statement of Professional Values, and three of its six tenets are relevant here:

1. "Adhere to the highest standard of accuracy and truth." Accuracy and truth are denied when the source of a message is a guarded secret.

2. Independence, as advised in the statement, is not maintained in this case. The public relations practitioner is told to "keep quiet" about the source rather than use his or her judgment as to the best approach to the issue.

3. Most important, the "loyalty" tenet commands that members "serve the public interest." Serving the public interest by providing an open and accurate flow of information is our duty and a virtue of public relations' benefit to society.

The practitioner here is asked to conceal information that would most likely serve the public interest (i.e., information about which community leaders and organizations are in favor of the airport extension).

The code Provisions offers specific guidance in this case under the core principle of disclosure of information (see PRSA Code, 2000, p. 10). Many argue that revealing sponsors is a responsibility inherent in building public trust. The practitioner in this case is asked to violate several guidelines regarding disclosure of information.

A code of ethics is a guideline for reasoning through a moral dilemma, an enactment of Kohlberg's (1969) conventional level of moral development in which one seeks to follow established rules of ethical behavior. Public relations would be better served if practitioners understood the reasons for making the moral decision alone, thereby operating at Kohlberg's highest level, the postconventional.

Deontology, based on moral norms of duty, includes codes of ethics, so it is a natural extension of this discussion. Deontology's focus on the universality of moral determinations concludes that to be valuable, communication has the inherent assumption of honesty. Lying or secrecy means that the lie works only if it is thought to be the truth—in this case, that the Citizens for Economic Progress is indeed a grassroots coalition of volunteers comprising concerned citizens. If lying were to be universalized, the credibility and structure of communication would break down, and truthful communication would become indistinguishable from the prattle of dishonesty and concealment.

When the intention is to deceive, one can conclude that such an action is unethical without regard to the justness of the actual issue involved. Even if a front group is created for a cause that is believed to be ethically acceptable, not disclosing the source of the message is inherently dishonest.

Deontology asks the decision maker to place himself in the role of those affected by the decision. If one can still support the decision from the vantages of varying publics, it is ethical. Could the public relations practitioner in this case determine that he or she would think it was acceptable to have the source of information concealed if he or she were among a receiving public?

Failure to disclose information is wrong because it does not maintain the relationships based on mutual respect and trust, which is vital in public relations. Nondisclosure denies the inherent dignity of people (publics) that deontology demands.

Consider if the same airport wanted to expand another runway in a few years—but the publics involved remembered this front group and believed misleading communication would again surround the issue. Dishonest activity might win the issue in one instance, but it fails to build relationships with publics, and those publics will often have a stake in future activities of the organization.

Morally, the public relations practitioner has many reasons to educate his or her boss, but that education must involve practical considerations.

The practitioner could explain that the truth regarding funding would invariably surface. When that happens a major crisis would ensue, publics would feel betrayed, and the city council would most likely vote against the expansion out of anger.

The practitioner could explain the potential negative consequences of not acting ethically and use examples from similar instances to reinforce the reality of the risk involved.

The practitioner should also have some solid ideas of how to replace the errant plan. Such an argument could begin, "The citizen support group is a great idea, so why don't we work to organize a real one, made of volunteers from area businesses?"

Reference

Kohlberg, L. (1969). Stage and sequence: The cognitive developmental approach to socialization. In D. A. Goslin (Ed.), *Handbook of socialization theory of research* (pp. 347-480). Chicago: Rand McNally.

By Shannon A. Bowen
Assistant Professor of Communication
University of Houston

Commentary 4
It Doesn't Pass the Smell Test

As someone who worked for seven chief executive officers (CEOs) at a public company over a 22-year period, there is only one response to the hypothetical boss of the small commercial airport located on the edge of town with a population of 250,000. It can only be, "We have to tell the truth." There is no alternative in these days of the post-Enron era.

Not providing all the facts about the source of the funding so that members of the city council will believe the grassroots initiative grew out of citizen concern for the development of the town is a grievous, if not unethical, error.

Holding back information from the public in this particular case doesn't pass the smell test. Over the long term, the information will undoubtedly find its way onto the front page of the local daily or weekly newspaper. So why hold it back?

From a practical point of view, and without even considering the ethics part of the situation, in this particular case the decision to suppress information is simply dead wrong.

From a career perspective, if the story gets out, the head of the small commercial airport and the public relations person will most likely find themselves out of a job for being less than professional. Just because the boss lacks ethics does not mean that the head of public relations has to go along with the plan to deceive the public.

Such a decision violates PRSA's Code of Ethics. The public relations person must have the strength to do what is right ethically. He or she must turn to his or her moral compass for direction. In my opinion, this kind of situation can no longer be described as a fairly routine act by public relations people even though it demonstrates the clash between the idealism of the code and the practical behavior of the professional.

In my investor relations class at the Newhouse School of Public Communications at Syracuse University, I stressed over and over again the importance of using your moral compass and being honest in your role as the chief investor relations person for a public company.

Leaving your moral compass in your desk drawer will cause the investor relations person to lose credibility almost immediately—not only within a given company but also in the wider investor community as well. It is no different for the public relations person.

At some companies, the public relations and the investor relations functions are handled under one umbrella, so having an ethical philosophy no matter which discipline one is working on is important.

If the small commercial airport were a public company listed on the New York Stock Exchange (NYSE) or National Association of Securities Dealers Automatic Quotations (NASDAQ), Regulation Fair Disclosure might also come into play. That regulation ensures that each investor receives the same information at the same time. This has completely changed the investor relations field. Fair Disclosure was mandated in October 2000 by the Securities and Exchange Commission so that the "individual investor is no longer going to be considered a secondary recipient of information."

If one wants to forget the fair disclosure regulation in this particular case, common sense should rule. Public relations people know many cases where the public relations professional went along with the boss to protect his or her job, and it was the wrong decision.

If one has to resign because of the unethical behavior of the boss, that is what has to be done regardless of the personal consequences. Sleeping soundly at night will be that person's reward.

The two other alternatives to be considered are (a) convince the boss to allow all the information to be disclosed, or (b) become a whistle-blower as we have seen in the Enron case.

"Now more than ever, CEOs need to be honest, substantive and possess the ability to build and restore confidence," according to panelists at a breakfast hosted by Stanton Crenshaw Communications last November. "Communicating from the Top: Lessons from Today's Leaders," an article in a recent issue of PRSA's monthly magazine, the *Public Relations Strategist*, addressed that forum.

Martin Jones, former CEO of Allied Domecq Spirits USA, said at the forum, "We have better educated publics, consumers, and analysts, and they want substance. They want the details, the results, and the facts. People are looking for honesty. They are looking for leaders who don't present a contrived identity."

More could be said regarding this particular case, but there is no question the head of the small commercial airport is out of line. The public relations person has to stand up to his or her boss and use his or her moral compass to change the situation. There is no other way.

I rest my case.

By William F. Doescher, President and CEO
The Doescher Group Ltd.
Scarsdale, New York

Journal of Mass Media Ethics, 17(2), 183–189

Book Reviews

This section is the last of four produced by guest editor Paul Martin Lester. We are grateful to Professor Lester for his experimentation with format and with content and for giving the editor a needed, if not deserved, break. We invite guest editors for theme issues of the book review section. Would you like our readers to know what's up in a specialized field? Contact the book review editor or editorial assistant with your ideas. As always, we seek suggestions for materials to be reviewed, and most particularly, we seek writers interested in writing reviews.

Editor: Deni Elliott
Practical Ethics Center
The University of Montana
Missoula, MT 59812
elliottd@mso.umt.edu

The Ethical Treatment of Entertainment Demands More Than Ethics for Dummies
A Review by Lawrence A. Wenner

Valenti, F. M. (2000). *More than a movie: Ethical decision making in the entertainment industry.* Boulder, CO: Westview. 256 pp., $20.00 (Pbk).

The gap in media ethics that F. Miguel Valenti's *More Than a Movie* addresses is a considerable one. The book's unique focus on the ethical considerations seen in creating film and television entertainment takes the reader on a voyage where "no ship has gone before" and sets it apart from journalism-centered treatments of media ethics. Although the voyage taken allows the passenger to see new ethical ports of call in intriguing ways, the excursion is also colored by being one "long strange trip."

As a Los Angeles–based producer, manager, and entertainment attorney, Valenti (no apparent relation to the Motion Picture Association of America's Jack Valenti) brings a set of relevant professional credentials to *More Than a Movie.* Having taught film business courses at Yale University, Valenti writes in a snappy style that is accessible to students. Nonetheless, in the book's introduction, he clearly states that this is not a textbook intended to be used as part of "formal classroom curriculum" and that is not "academic in nature" (p. xx). Intentions aside, Valenti consciously uses a voice aimed at getting through to students who are preparing themselves for creative careers in film and television. In short, he writes for the film school audience, stating, "this book is *not* concerned primarily with the *business* ethics of the entertainment industry," but rather the "ethics of *content*" (p. xix).

The focus on the ethical dimensions involved in the creation of popular entertainment content makes this book unique. But so too does the interweaving of comments from a cast of 13 entertainment industry professionals, which includes writers, directors, producers, casting directors, publicity agents, independent filmmakers, and studio executives. That the book has many voices from the streets of film and television production gives it veracity for the student reader; it helps it work against the professor "preaching" stereotype that may be associated with media ethics textbooks.

Valenti's own writing forms the backbone of the book. His voice is also amplified by contributions from others that help stimulate ethical reflection. Here, for example, former *New York Times* television critic Les Brown writes thoughtfully about the social effects and economic priorities in today's media, *TV Guide*'s Neil Hickey considers the problems of television violence for children, and documentary filmmaker Martin Koughan gives compelling examples of hype and deception in television newsmagazines. In other treatments, Jack Pitman writes about the cultural imperialism seen in Hollywood content and business practices; Ted Pease chronicles the history of censorship, the Hays code, and blacklisting in Hollywood; and Annette Insdorf questions the progress that has been made when sexual stereotyping moves from "boys with toys" to "babes with bullets."

Although all of these contributing authors make concise and accessible approaches to their topics, perhaps the most useful contribution was a fairly extensive foreword written by film director Peter Bogdanovich (*The Last Picture Show*). He frames his remarks by saying that "in sophisticated circles today, the mere mention of 'ethics in filmmaking' is bound to get a cynical laugh, one that says there aren't any" (p. vii). Bogdanovich poses that filmmakers cannot be excused from their moral responsibilities, especially at times such as now that he finds largely amoral. Although he argues that the "glorification of gangsters and outlaws is virtually a Hollywood tradition," (p. x), he raises important issues that make the reader think differentially about treatments of violence. For Bogdanovich the trick is in finding "moral authority" in portrayals of violence and avoiding inadvertent decisions that do not make heroes out of misguided purveyors of aggression.

From Bogdanovich's foreword, Valenti launches into the larger mission of the book. Valenti's approach is ultimately pragmatic. He reassures the reader that he is not concerned with the "academic analysis of the complex world of higher ethical principles," and he argues for an approach appropriate to the "situational ethics" that dominates Hollywood decision making (pp. xx–xxi). Because of this, Valenti avoids "dictating" morality and focuses, rather, on the nurturing of what he calls an "ethical choice reflex" (p. xxiii) in budding filmmakers. The approach is centered in having the reader consider scenarios and exercises as "ethical gymnastics" (p. xxi) in hypothetical narratives of creative disputes that students might encounter in the world of film and television production.

What is so striking in the framing chapters is Valenti's hypersensitivity to the fear that any approach that does not allow for situational relativism will be a turn-off to the reader. Although Valenti indeed may be right in estimating (or underestimating) his audience, the basic approach would most likely be viewed as a slippery slope and disheartening to any Kantian ethicist. The reader of the book is positioned as "the skeptic," and in fact Valenti uses the strategy of dialogue with a constructed skeptic to first argue for ethics in entertainment content and then to introduce some of the philosophical underpinnings of ethics in a nonthreatening way to the reader. In these exchanges, the skeptic is colored as terminally bored with the prospects of philosophy and incensed at the prospect of wrestling with ethics in the doing of art. A typical exchange follows:

The Skeptic: Why "ethics?" Ethics stifle creativity, and have no place in the world of art. They keep creators from pushing the edge of the envelope, and developing into unique voices. They hew off the rough edges of new creation, so necessary for growth.

Response: Ethics in and of themselves do not stifle creativity. If you know an ethical choice when you see one, it can vastly increase your power to develop art. If "the unexamined life is not worth living," arguably, the unexamined creation may not be worth creating (p. xv).

Such dialogues are used with mixed success. Some just tend to reinforce what might be called Valenti's "ethics for dummies." Even the naming of one of the dialogues in his "ethical primer" section—"Dead White Greeks and Why They Matter"—illustrates the push–pull that Valenti has with the material and his audience. One comes away wondering if a less pithy, straight-ahead approach might have reached the target audience with more success and less insult.

The strongest chapters in Valenti's book are those that grow from the work of Mediascope in the areas of violence, stereotypes, substance use, and sex. Indeed, Valenti's project is touted on the back cover as "emerging"

out of Mediascope, a national nonprofit research and policy organization that has an admirable record in pro-social media strategies (see http://www.mediascope.org). Unfortunately, Valenti has chosen to wrap the ethics connection to this important work in a section titled, "All You Need to Make a Movie Is a Girl and a Gun. ..." Still, the violence chapter in particular does a good job of demonstrating a series of ethical hot-button choices that stem from the National Television Violence Study. He considers the consequences involved in the choice of perpetrator of violence; the choice of victim; the reason for violence; the use of weapons; the uses of realism and humor; and the portrayal of consequences, rewards, and punishment for violence. The treatment here adds much to more simplistic harm assessments made in other media ethics texts.

Similarly, Valenti's treatment of the complexity of ethical choice that surrounds the use of stereotyping in entertainment narratives adds much to existing treatments. He not only gives good reasons for the economical necessities of stereotype in short narrative forms, but also poses effective examples of alternatives to stereotyping of gender, race, and occupation. The thoughtfulness of this treatment is mirrored in Valenti's chapter on sexual portrayals. He advances the discussion of ethical choice by framing sexual violence as a public health issue. Another strong component of this chapter is his attention to considering sexual responsibility in the course of dramatic development, giving extended attention to the special case of teen sex.

Although these latter areas are touched on in other media ethics texts, Valenti's insider view of real life Hollywood production processes reaches out to a more useful applied ethics for the student filmmaker. He adds to the discussion in two areas that often receive little treatment by media ethicists. By giving equal attention to the ethical issues surrounding the portrayal of substance use and abuse, Valenti heightens focus on issues of harm that may come from inadvertently glorifying smoking, drinking, and drug use in entertainment narratives. In addition, with the rise of reality programming on prime-time television schedules and more and more feature docudrama coloring the landscape, Valenti opens the door for effective discussion of ethical choices inherent in dramatizing something that is based on a true story or based on history told from a certain point of view.

In sum, Valenti's *More Than a Movie* makes some real contributions to applied ethics as it relates to creative decisions in popular entertainment media. Clearly, the work breaks new ground. That's the good news. The bad news may be the "ethics for dummies" tone that frames other elements that are thoughtfully presented. The situational relativism that is embraced may be too much for some users to take. Still, because the work gets at ethical crossroads little seen in media ethics, *More Than a Movie* belongs on the bookshelf of anyone committed to teaching media ethics in a way that goes beyond journalism ethics. Regardless of whether the book itself is used, the important issues it raises will surely make their way into many a media ethics course.

❏ *Lawrence A. Wenner is the Von der Ahe Professor of Communication and Ethics in the College of Communication and Fine Arts at Loyola Marymount University in Los Angeles.*

A Plea for Humane Cyberspace
A Review by John P. Ferré

Hamelink, C. (2000). *The Ethics of Cyberspace.* Thousand Oaks, CA: Sage. 220 pp., $24.95 (Pbk).

Just a few years ago, the prevailing attitude about the governance of cyberspace was that there should be none—or more precisely, that cyberspace should be politically libertarian and economically laissez-faire. This thinking continues, of course, but concerns about pornography, viruses, identity fraud, and hacking have put it in decline. New approaches to the governance of cyberspace are emerging, approaches that range from voluntarism to government regulation. The more thoughtful among these approaches take democratic processes and human rights into account. This is where Cees Hamelink, Professor of International Communication at the University of Amsterdam, weighs in.

Hamelink dismisses most ethical reasoning as authoritarian or irrelevant, a mismatch for an increasingly multicultural, pluralist, and interconnected world. "Although personal, professional and corporate moral choices are of paramount importance," Hamelink says, "the most decisive questions are issues of social ethics. Even if all personal, professional and corporate users of cyberspace were to behave in virtuous and decent ways, this would not automatically mean we would have a decent society" (p. 52). A decent society is one that respects the rights of all human beings, rights affirmed in the Universal Declaration of Human Rights by the United Nations General Assembly in 1948, and that includes all of its members in an ongoing process of decision making over issues that affect them.

Cyberspace governed with respect for human rights and participatory democracy, according to the author, would demonstrate equality, security, and freedom. There would be universal access; no one could collect information about anyone else without public accountability; and all people would be free to express themselves and to gather knowledge. These are high ideals certainly, and high-priced ones, too, as Hamelink acknowledges in his calculation that universal access by itself could cost as much as $100 billion a year for 10 years. But ethics is about choosing rightly. Hamelink points out that this figure "represents some 11 percent of the world's annual spending on military projects, some 22 percent of total annual spending on narcotic drugs, and compares to the annual spending on alcoholic drinks in Europe alone" (p. 95). Like any shift in social priorities, the ethical governance of cyberspace would be expensive, but possible.

Hamelink's vision of a humane and democratic cyberspace does represent a sea change from the market-centered cyberspace that we have today. Global policies of deregulation, privatization, and conglomeration have insured maximum freedom for market forces and minimum public intervention. Cyberspace is controlled by corporations that are profit oriented, with only the most egregious excesses addressed though ineffective processes of self-regulation. Driven by unchecked market imperatives, cyberspace has had four negative social consequences:

- Exclusion: Internet access is increasing dramatically, but unevenly. Four out of five users live in developed countries, and increases in access in the Northern Hemisphere, Australia, and New Zealand far outpace increases in most of the Southern Hemisphere. Prospects for what Hamelink calls "serious social exclusion" run high.
- Lack of diversity: Most Web sites are designed to serve English-speaking, educated, and economically comfortable people. That leaves the cultural and information needs of most people not served and thus depletes the public sphere of a broad range of perspective and expression.
- Censorship: The Internet's potential to support discussions and debates on important social issues is dampened by state censorship and by the self-censorship of Internet companies. Copyright rules and laws on business defamation contribute to the chilling effect.
- Invasions of privacy: Headlines about Carnivore, the FBI's computer system that monitors Internet traffic and copies e-mail, and about the surreptitious profiling of physicians' prescriptions by IMS Canada are but two reminders of the increasing surveillance of individuals by government and business. Such surveillance, as Hamelink reminds us, is performed routinely in the home and in the workplace without broad deliberation about the social consequences, not to mention public consent.

The Ethics of Cyberspace would serve well as a supplementary text in a communication ethics course. Its dismissal of deontological and teleological theories of ethics in favor of processes of participatory democracy is too sweeping. Its advocacy of education and civic movements as an antidote to governance by private enterprise is underdeveloped. But its placement of cyberspace in a social and economic context is sound, its argument for humane and democratic principles and processes is provocative, and its call for deliberate and deliberative policy-making is reasonable.

❏ *John P. Ferré is Professor of Communication at the University of Louisville.*

Books Received

Best, J. (2001). *Damned lies and statistics: Untangling numbers from the media, politicians, and activists.* Berkeley, CA: University of California Press. 199 pp., $19.95 (Hbk).

Bunker, M. D. (2001). *Critiquing free speech: First Amendment theory and the challenge of interdisciplinarity.* Mahwah, NJ: Lawrence Erlbaum Associates, Inc. 206 pp., $39.95 (Hbk).

Chin, E. (2001). *Purchasing power: Black kids and American consumer culture.* Minneapolis: University of Minnesota Press. 272 pp., $17.95 (Pbk).

Ebo, B. (Ed). (2001). *Cyberimperialism?: Global relations in the new electronic frontier.* Westport, CT: Praeger. 280 pp., $68.50 (Hbk).

Jensen, G., & Wiest, A. (Eds). (2001). *War in the age of technology: Myriad faces of modern armed conflict.* New York: New York University Press. 380 pp., $65.00 (Hbk). $21.00 (Pbk).

Merrill, J., Gade, P., & Blevens, F. (2001). *Twilight of press freedom: The rise of people's journalism.* Mahwah, NJ: Lawrence Erlbaum Associates, Inc. 230 pp., $49.95 (Hbk). $24.50 (Pbk).

Mitchell, C. (Ed.). (2000). *Women and radio: Airing differences.* New York: Routledge. 295 pp., $26.95 (Pbk).

Morgan, D., & Promey, S. (Eds.). (2001). *The visual culture of American religions.* Berkeley: University of California Press. 441 pp., $60.00 (Hbk). $29.95 (Pbk).

Weinberg, A., & Weinberg, L. (Eds.). (2001). *The muckrakers.* Champaign: University of Illinois Press. 450 pp., $19.95 (Pbk).

Wood, A., & Smith, M. (2001). *Online communication: Linking technology, identity, and culture.* Mahwah, NJ: Lawrence Erlbaum Associates, Inc. 230 pp., $27.50 (Pbk).

SUBSCRIPTION ORDER FORM

Please ❑ enter ❑ renew my subscription to:

JOURNAL OF MASS MEDIA ETHICS
EXPLORING QUESTIONS OF MEDIA MORALITY
Volume 17, 2002, Quarterly — ISSN 0890–0523/Online ISSN 1532–7728

SUBSCRIPTION PRICES PER VOLUME:

Individual:	Institution:	Online Only:
❑ $35.00 US/Canada	❑ $320.00 US/Canada	❑ $31.50 Individual
❑ $65.00 All Other Countries	❑ $350.00 All Other Countries	❑ $288.00 Institution

Subscriptions are entered on a calendar-year basis only and must be paid in advance in U.S. currency—check, credit card, or money order. Prices for subscriptions include postage and handling. Journal prices expire 12/31/02. **NOTE**: Institutions must pay institutional rates. Individual subscription orders are welcome if prepaid by credit card or personal check. **Online access is included with individual subscriptions.**

❑   **Check Enclosed** (U.S. Currency Only)   Total Amount Enclosed $_____

❑   **Charge My**: ❑ VISA   ❑ MasterCard   ❑ AMEX   ❑ Discover

Card Number _____   Exp. Date_____/_____

Signature _____
(Credit card orders cannot be processed without your signature.)

PRINT CLEARLY for proper delivery. STREET ADDRESS/SUITE/ROOM # REQUIRED FOR DELIVERY.

Name_____

Address_____

City/State/ Zip+4_____

Daytime Phone #_____E-mail address_____
Prices are subject to change without notice.

Please note: A $20.00 penalty will be charged against customers providing checks that must be returned for payment. This assessment will be made only in instances when problems in collecting funds are directly attributable to customer error.

For information about online subscriptions, visit our website at *www.erlbaum.com*

Mail orders to: **Lawrence Erlbaum Associates, Inc.,** Journal Subscription Department
10 Industrial Avenue, Mahwah, NJ 07430; **(201) 258–2200; FAX (201) 760–3735; journals@erlbaum.com**

LIBRARY RECOMMENDATION FORM

Detach and forward to your librarian.

❑ I have reviewed the description of the *Journal of Mass Media Ethics* and would like to recommend it for acquisition.

JOURNAL OF MASS MEDIA ETHICS
EXPLORING QUESTIONS OF MEDIA MORALITY
Volume 17, 2002, Quarterly — ISSN 0890–0523/Online ISSN 1532–7728

Institutional Rate: ❑ **$320.00** (US & Canada)   ❑ **$350.00** (All Other Countries)

Name_____Title_____

Institution/Department_____

Address _____

E-Mail Address_____
Librarians, please send your orders directly to LEA or contact from your subscription agent.

Lawrence Erlbaum Associates, Inc., Journal Subscription Department
10 Industrial Avenue, Mahwah, NJ 07430; **(201) 258–2200; FAX (201) 760–3735; journals@erlbaum.com**

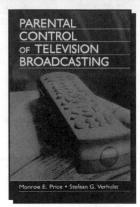

STAY TUNED
A History of American Broadcasting, Third Edition
Christopher H. Sterling
George Washington University
John Michael Kittross
K\E\G Associates
A Volume in LEA's Communication Series

"Stay Tuned is the best single-volume history of American broadcasting in print!"

—**Michael C. Keith**
Boston College

Since its initial publication in 1978, *Stay Tuned* has been recognized as the most comprehensive and useful single-volume history of American broadcasting and electronic media available. This third edition has been thoroughly revised and updated to bring the story of American broadcasting forward to the 21st century, affording readers not only the history of the most important and pervasive institution affecting our society, but also providing a contextual transition to the Internet and other modern media.

The enthusiasm of authors Christopher Sterling and John Michael Kittross is apparent as they lead readers through the development of American electronic mass media, from the first electrical communication (telegraph and telephone); through radio and television; to the present convergence of media, business entities, programming, and delivery systems, including the Internet. Their presentation is engaging, as well as informative, promoting an interest in history and making the connections between the developments of yesterday and the industry of today.

Features of this third edition include:
* chronological and topical tables of contents;
* new material reflecting modern research in the field;
* a new chapter describing historical developments from 1988 through to the current day;
* an expanded bibliography, including Web site and museum listings;
* an updated and expanded glossary and chronology; and
* extensive statistical data of the development of television and radio stations, networks, advertising, programming, audiences, and other aspects of broadcasting.

Designed for use in undergraduate and graduate courses on the history of American mass media, broadcasting, and electronic media, *Stay Tuned* also fits well into mass communication survey courses as an introduction to electronic media topics. As a chronicle of American broadcasting, this volume is also engaging reading for anyone interested in old radio, early television, and the origins and development of American broadcasting.

Contents: The Context of Broadcasting. The Prehistory of Broadcasting (to 1919). The Beginnings of Broadcasting (1920-1926). The Coming of Commercialism (1926-1933). Radio's Golden Age (1934-1941). Radio Goes to War (1941-1945). Era of Great Change (1945-1952). The Age of Television (1952-1960). Accommodation and Adjustment (1961-1976). Challenge and Competition (1977-1988). Change and Evolution (1988-2001). Lessons From the Past for the Future. **Appendices:** A Short Chronology of American Broadcasting. Glossary. Historical Statistics on Broadcasting. Selected Bibliography.
0-8058-2624-6 [cloth] / 2002 / 1000pp. / $59.95
Prices are subject to change without notice.

Lawrence Erlbaum Associates, Inc.
10 Industrial Ave., Mahwah, NJ 07430–2262
201–258–2200; 1–800–926–6579; fax 201–760–3735
orders@erlbaum.com; www.erlbaum.com

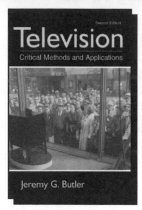

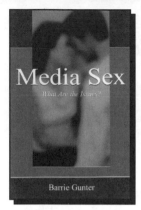

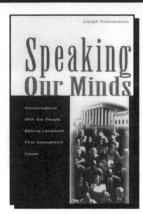